I Kept My Word

The Personal Promise Between a
World War II Army Private and His Captain
About What Really Happened to Glenn Miller

Clarence B. Wolfe

as told to Susan Goodrich Giffin

Bloomington, IN   Milton Keynes, UK

authorHOUSE®

AuthorHouse™
1663 Liberty Drive, Suite 200
Bloomington, IN 47403
www.authorhouse.com
Phone: 1-800-839-8640

AuthorHouse™ UK Ltd.
500 Avebury Boulevard
Central Milton Keynes, MK9 2BE
www.authorhouse.co.uk
Phone: 08001974150

First published by AuthorHouse 10/10/2006

ISBN: 1-4259-6950-X (sc)
ISBN: 1-4259-6951-8 (dj)

Library of Congress Control Number: 2006908964

Printed in the United States of America
Bloomington, Indiana

This book is printed on acid-free paper.

To Glenn Miller fans everywhere

...and to my family

Private 1st Class Clarence B. Wolfe
U. S. Army
134th AAA Battalion
Battery D

Preface

It is one thing to entertain military troops in large tents or on open-air stages, but it is yet another to stir the souls of countless soldiers mired in muddy foxholes and marching numbly in sub-zero weather as bombs burst around them. That was the miracle of Glenn Miller, whose big band sound circled the globe during World War II.

This book tells the true story of how the remarkable talent of Glenn Miller suddenly fell silent. This story has never been told until now. For the past 62 years, I have participated in a conspiracy of silence with Captain Lawrence Foley, commanding officer of Gun Battery D of the 134th AAA Battalion since the bright, clear morning Miller went missing. You see – Miller wasn't missing at all. The Captain and I knew exactly what happened to him. *I Kept My Word* is that story.

Now the Captain is deceased, and evidently he kept his word to the end. I'm sure he was as heartsick as I was that we were involved in any way.

However, now that I am drawing closer to the end of my life, and as the only living person directly involved in – though not responsible for – Miller's death, I believe it is time to pay my debt to his fans by breaking my promise.

Over the years since Miller's disappearance and death, many theories have surfaced to lay claim to the truth about this great loss. In addition to their fascination – and occasional preposterousness – these theories indicate a yearning on the part of his fans to know the truth, once and for all. I hope that my revelations in this book will put this matter to rest.

Finally, this is not just the story of what really happened to Glenn Miller; it is also my story of service and survival in World War II and my dramatic rescue from behind enemy lines. I choose to believe I survived more than one brush with death for a purpose, and that is to share the truth about Glenn Miller's demise.

I have withdrawn from my own bank of vivid memories the description of events and experiences in which I was involved while serving with the 134ᵗʰ AAA Battalion in World War II. In no way, have I intended for any information published herein to cast shadows on anyone else involved in these events and experiences, unless deliberately stated. In some cases, I preferred not to state names, so as to avoid any potential embarrassment to their surviving families. Above all, to the best of my ability, I have told the truth of events as I witnessed them. When all is said and done, I must be true to myself first by telling the truth as I know it.

—CBW

Acknowledgements

Putting a book together is an awesome undertaking. At one point, I said to my editor "I feel wrung out." I had opened up a huge storehouse of memories and images, some of which I surely wish I could forget. Some were truly painful experiences; and memories of them still reduce me to tears. Some memories triggered others that I thought I had forgotten, and yet others gave me a good belly laugh.

This effort is far too daunting for someone like me who has never written a book. Therefore, I wish to extend my heartfelt appreciation to a few people that helped me along the way.

First of all, I never would have written this book without the early encouragement of Dave Horn, formerly of the Herald Times in Bloomington. I guess it's best to say that he inspired me, but he also made me realize the value of what I have to say.

I would like to recognize the lifelong love and support of my daughter, Darlene, and my late daughter, Donna.

To my editor, Susan Goodrich Giffin, I cannot adequately express my gratitude for her diligence in conducting exhaustive research on various topics and for meticulously crafting my thoughts. In both areas, she went way beyond the call of duty and made me realize the gifts she possesses as a writer and an editor.

I would like to thank members of Battery D of the 134th Battalion – or their families – that helped us piece together certain parts of the war puzzle. We sincerely appreciate all the efforts of Bill and Rita McLaughlin to keep tabs on the 134th and bring the 134th together for reunions. With their assistance, we located several members of Battery D or Headquarters or their families – Gilbert "Gibby" Davis, Ed Shanahan, Pete Hall, Earl Gamble, George Delaney and Richard Flora, author of the Battalion's "Madcap Memories" (some of which I have used to fill in blanks of my own story). Also, John Finegan's son, John, Mrs. Lawrence (Janet) Foley, Mrs. Salvatore (Phyllis) Rancatore and Mrs. William (Betty Miller), thank you for stories, information and photographs.

Special thanks to John Pfeister's sons, John and Jeff Pfeister, long-time students of the Battle of the Bulge and other wartime activities of that era. They raised questions that got me thinking, fueled our efforts with enthusiasm and provided Susan with photographs, maps and stories that helped her put my experiences into perspective.

I would be remiss if I did not thank four other people: Carol Ann Francis for her kind assistance, Gib Van Horn for his encouragement, Lou Malcomb, Librarian at Indiana University in Bloomington for her research efforts on my behalf and Vid Beldavs at AuthorHouse for introducing me to my editor and for wisely counseling me throughout the publishing process.

I salute all of you for a job well done!

-CBW

Table of Contents

World War II was the most destructive human endeavor in history. Battles were fought on every continent and involved more than 60 countries, affecting roughly three-quarters of the world's population.

Mitchell G. Bard, Ph.D.

Introduction

When I first received a call from Clarence B. Wolfe, relating his interest in breaking his silence about the death of an important celebrity during World War II, there must have been interference on the line. I eventually learned that he mentioned Glenn Miller, but that name did not become apparent or his story until I received a letter and background information from Mr. Wolfe a few days later. Needless to say, I was greatly intrigued by the impact such a story would have on Glenn Miller fans around the world.

From our first contact, I noticed something unique about Clarence "CB" Wolfe. He is direct, forthright and honest. His memory is sharp, and his desire to tell the truth is the driving force in his life. That he kept a secret for 62 years gives a powerful clue to his integrity. His compulsion to reveal his secret before he dies is equally impressive, for without his story, the world would never know what really happened to Glenn Miller, dispelling all lingering doubts

I believe CB's memories are so sharp because keeping such an incredible secret all these years has allowed him to hold fast to all the memories that surround it. He retains an incredible ability to explain events and equipment in detail.

It has been a privilege and an honor to work with CB on this important project, to hear stories about his service and survival in World War II that he has never told anyone before and to get a rare glimpse at the personal side of wartime drama.

This book is a page-turner. In it you will find heartbreak and humor, the gamut of wartime emotions and sufficient danger and disaster that engenders respect for the risk that men and women take in service for their country.

-Susan Goodrich Giffin
Editor

Chapter 1

Clarence B. Wolfe

One must have a good memory
to be able to keep the promises one makes.
Friedrich Nietzsche
1844-1900

You could say that my parents – Ben and Ella Wolfe – were close, because they produced 11 babies to prove it. Born, June 21, 1924 in Clay City, Indiana, I was the youngest. Mother evidently reared healthy children, because none of my siblings died young. The baby in the family, I am now 82. I walk three miles a day and feel not a day over 50.

My mother's maiden name was Foxworthy. Her family was very smart, and you knew it just as soon as you entered into a conversation with one of them. Only two became professors, but that was only because the family lacked sufficient funds to send the others through schools of higher learning.

My dad had only a second grade education, but he was very smart. With no effort at all, he could solve any problem that we brought home from school.

He had a gift, too, that his father handed down to him. He could cure many ailments in children without the use of medications or magic potions. I remember seeing women wheeling buggies up the path with their babies screaming in pain and, it seemed, almost on the verge of death.

Dad took the baby to the kitchen and closed the door. Once, I watched through the keyhole as he carefully cradled the baby's head in his hand and performed his healing by gently blowing around the baby's face.

After what seemed mere minutes, the screaming stopped and Dad returned the baby to its grateful mother. I never saw any mother return her baby to him for another treatment.

Dad always promised to pass the secret to his youngest (yours truly), but he never got the opportunity, so the Wolfe healing powers died with him years later.

As for my father, I felt sorry for him, because he worked hard all his life, ending up with 11 hungry kids to feed, and his own health that was in a purely awful state. He could heal babies, but he had no money to go to a doctor to take care of his own ailments.

Way back when, the Wolfe family was well off, but then tuberculosis hit, and there went the money. What is unbelievable is that not one of us children ever contracted TB, but back then families helped each other. We were never allowed to kiss on the mouth, for instance. That was my Dad's idea and without a doubt that explains, in part, why we never had colds or caught TB.

That Depression was a son of a bitch that affected young and old alike. We were dirt poor, but we didn't know it. Everyone around us was the same way, so we just thought it was how everybody lived. It is difficult to understand how poor people were back then.

I never had any clothes that fit me. They were always hand-me-downs from my older brothers (there were eight boys in the family). My nickname back then was "Bag", because that's how all my clothes fit.

We lived on a farm, and we raised corn and wheat. Clay City, a rural town, was our official address, but our farm was closer to Coal City, named – quite appropriately – for the coal that was so plentiful in the area; it was even above ground in some places. It was great coal, too. The town hasn't changed one bit over the years, except for the addition of a post office.

Whenever Dad took his harvest of corn or wheat to the mill for grinding, and the mill would not offer even a nickel a bushel, because there was no demand. I would sit in the back of the wagon so sad and cry like a baby without fully understanding why.

Here I am in the middle.
Don't we look like a ragtag bunch?

At one time, our farm had been an Indian village, and as a kid I gathered buckets of Indian artifacts – tomahawks, arrowheads, pipes and spears. Instead of moving to a new location when the land gave out, the Indians just continued to farm it, and to this day that land will produce only weeds.

Corn seemed to be their mainstay. They could distill into hard liquor or grind it into flour. Liquor was more important to them than flour, of course, for trading purposes.

There were still two Indians left when I was a kid. Next to the mill, where Dad would take his grain for grinding, was a creamery. There stood the two Indians. They never spoke a word. They just stood there and looked. Maybe they were trying to figure out how they lost so much that was once theirs. At night, they would steal back into the deep forest. No one ever located their campsite.

One day they just didn't show up at the creamery, and we never saw them again. Strange, they just vanished.

I believe they were killed with kindness. You see everyone back then had a cold that lasted all winter. I mean, these were real barkers. The town ladies felt sorry for the Indians, as they had absolutely no food and no way of getting any.

The Indians had what we would call specialists; some were hunters, some farmers and others made weapons. And still others were just plain bums that kept the fires burning when everything was wet.

These two Indians, therefore, had no training or experience in hunting or gathering food. The townspeople knew this, of course, and saved their food scraps for the Indians. No doubt, this food was infected with germs, and the Indians had no defense against them. As a result, they died. I realize this is an assumption, but it makes the most sense to me. The Army had stripped the Indians of all their weapons and tools for the purpose of starving them to death and it worked.

Moving on

I left home when I was 15. I could tell I was a burden and the thrill of having children around was over for both my parents, so I left.

A string of events then changed my life dramatically. The two brothers closest to me in age knocked up a mother and her daughter. My father had to pay them money he did not have.

Well, I ran into the daughter on Main Street one Saturday night. I bought some rubbers [condoms] and took her into the alley, where I used up the whole supply. I was a horny 16-year-old, if you haven't figured that out already.

The next day, I shot a couple of squirrels and sold them so I could purchase more rubbers for a second go-round. Well, here she came down the street, but something was different. Her belly looked all swelled up. She grabbed my arm and took me into the alley.

"I'm knocked up and you and I got to get married!" she informed.

4

"I'll think about it," I said, as I fled the scene. [I later learned that she had strapped a pillow to her waist.]

What was I to do? That is when the idea of going to Detroit came to mind.

I asked Pop if he could give me $5.00, so I could visit my brother, Paul, and his wife, who had moved to Detroit. The Greyhound bus ticket cost $3.50. Somehow Pop got the Model A started and off to Brazil [Indiana] we went.

I was so damned happy to leave, I believe I forgot to say good-bye. Thank God my stomach was so shrunk that I never got hungry, plus I figured I should save the $1.50 left over after I purchased the ticket.

The big city

My eyes were as big as hubcaps when I arrived in Detroit. The cars, streetcars, pretty girls and the sounds of the city overwhelmed me. "This is for me," I said to myself. I relished the idea of new experiences, new people and a new environment.

Paul and his family were suffering a great deal from the Depression. When I arrived at their place, they had already eaten, but they offered me their leftovers. I gratefully accepted, only to learn that those would be my meals until I got settled on my own.

The Depression had a profound effect on me. As unbelievable as it sounds, every time I sat down to eat, I hesitated, thinking I was eating food that someone else needed more than I did. I never told anyone this until now.

They let me sleep in their basement. This might sound cruel today, but I was so happy to be more or less on my own, it did not matter to me. Indeed, I was very grateful. At 15, a person could not get a job, so it was pretty rough going.

I still had the $1.50, but I knew that I had to find work. My brother lived at 7 Mile Road and John R, so I would walk to Highland Park every morning, checking every business and factory. It was summer, but before I knew it, here came winter, and I still had not found a job. It was getting cold, and I had no warm clothes.

One day, I lucked out, getting a job at a greasy spoon washing dishes at 10 cents an hour. Of course, I was grateful for the job, but I also figured that working in a food establishment, however lowly, I would always have food. Wrong! I was not allowed to eat there, as the owner insisted I use my meager wages to buy whatever food I wanted. I was 6'2" and weighed 128 pounds. If you ever want to lose weight, it's simple: just don't eat.

I finally got around the owner's order by eating the food that people left on their plates before it had a chance to end up in the garbage can. It must not have hurt me, as I managed to put on a couple of pounds. I had always had a problem keeping my pants up, as I had no belly.

Across the street from Paul's house lived a family that had one little girl. The mother was cute as a button and while sitting on the porch, she would show me the better parts of her body. Well, it didn't take long before we were much closer.

One night while in her bed, up the stairs thundered her husband. I had only one escape option. Out the window I went, landing in a prickly barbary bush below. I had needles all over because my pants were in my hand! To this day, I still have one needle lodged in my leg. It's a reminder to be careful where I sleep!

Well, it took more trouble with women to eventually get me fired from the greasy spoon and into a better job. I'll spare you the details.

With spring around the corner, my job was pouring boiling asphalt on the rooftops of buildings, some of which were high, at least by standards back then. I didn't complain, because I was making 12 cents an hour.

Not too long after that, I lucked out when I found a job working in a tool and die shop at 56 cents an hour! I was rich! I remember walking to Highland Park. As I was walking down Woodward Avenue, the main thoroughfare, suddenly the crotch in the only pair of pants I owned broke loose. I had to walk the rest of the way with my legs more or less crossed. Except for the pant legs, everything else was flapping in the breeze!

My timing was great, because all this happened right in front of J. C. Penney's. I will never forget how wonderful those new pants felt. They were my first pair of new pants, ever! They fit perfectly and they cost $1.98.

My job at the tool and die shop was a dream. I was put off alone in the welding shop and there I did a lot of experimenting. Back then, it seemed that the government didn't care about experience; they just paid factories to fill them with hired workers. The body count was more important than any experience the workers had.

Drafted!

Well, all good things eventually come to an end. I was drafted in 1943 and ordered to report. My brother was good enough to drive me part way to the railroad station in downtown Detroit. I walked the rest of the way, getting there on time. I carried no suitcase, because I had nothing to put in one.

I did not tell my folks that I was drafted or went into the Army, but I did write to them after a while. To me, going to war would be another great experience. I looked forward to going into the Army, because other than acquiring new experiences, I knew I would eat. This meant a lot to me, because I wasn't eating well before I was drafted.

I don't know how many men felt like I did about being drafted. I had no fear of being killed, because my thoughts just didn't travel in that direction.

The train took me to Texas, and eventually I ended up at Camp Wallace. That first night many of the new draftees sobbed after the lights went out. I figured they must have had great loving families, because their tears etched their sadness at leaving them behind.

At one point, we were given a written test. I really didn't try hard, but I somehow must have done great on my test, because I was put into the category with Michigan State seniors that entered the army as buck sergeants. They were ROTC Reserve Army.

This meant that I was put into the range section where all the highly secret equipment was used in the training. I was amazed. These guys all had training in this field, and I knew absolutely nothing about it. I caught some of them smirking at my presence, and that made me try harder to learn. I must have learned something, because some of the same guys that had looked down their noses at me tapped me for information later.

One day, while stationed at Camp Wallace, I had 11 teeth filled without the benefit of novocaine. Oh, the pain! When I left the building, an old WW I general was waiting for me to salute him. The SOB was so old he could barely stand up. The pain somehow affected my arms so badly that I couldn't raise my arm to complete the salute so I ducked my head and grabbed an eyebrow to get my hand up for a salute.

That old bastard knew GIs would be leaving the dentist office in pain and could not salute, so he would write them up. It's truly amazing that we won World War I with the likes of those men in command.

One day I was called into the placement officer's quarters, and I thought, 'What the hell did I do?' You see, when you were called into his office, part of your ass would stay in there. To my surprise, the officer asked me if I wanted to attend officers' training school.

"If you read my school history, you would know that I shouldn't even be here," I replied.

At this, he merely smiled and dismissed me. I stayed with the group until the training period ended. Then the rest of the group returned to Michigan State University and received their commissions.

From Camp Wallace, I caught a train to the Great Lakes Training Center in Chicago. I was about to become a gunner with a newly formed outfit known as the 134th AAA Battalion that was part of the coast artillery.

So, what, you ask, does my mundane early life have to do with World War II, Glenn Miller or anything else? Well, I wanted to paint a picture of what the average draftee was like going off to the big war. Most of us were average – farm boys, small-town lads and a few city slickers. None of us had experienced life in a big way, and few of us had traveled beyond our hometowns.

By the time we were all scooped up to serve, there were over 11 million of us in just the Army and Army Air Force alone. That's a lot of innocent young men going off to serve their country, some brave, but most scared to death.

Over 300,000 of us would die, and another 135,000 captured or missing. I recently heard that thousands of MIAs are still unaccounted for from World War II!

Chapter 2

World War II

*You cannot simultaneously
prevent and prepare for war.*
Albert Einstein
1879-1955

It wasn't until we started putting together information for this book that I learned a lot about the war in which I fought and almost died several times. You know, when you are in the midst of war as enormous in scale as World War II, you don't stop to wonder what the generals are thinking or where this country or that one will invade next. You are too busy keeping yourself alive!

Now, looking at the war from a veteran's perspective, it's amazing how the generals put it together. It was a massive undertaking that engulfed most of the world. The logistics are beyond my comprehension.

Nonetheless, let's take a brief look at what started this war that would eventually cause more death and destruction than any war before or since. Although pre-war problems arose in the Far East before they did in Europe, for the purposes of my story, we will confine this brief overview of World War II to the United Kingdom and parts of the European continent.

What causes people to go to war? Thanks probably to those World War I generals that were more consumed with spilling blood than sparing it, there were plenty of unresolved issues left over from that war, hard feelings that festered and finally erupted.

The fighting in World War I came to a halt in 1918 when an armistice was signed. The following year, the Allied forces, 29 in all if you count just the British Empire and not all the countries under its rule (Canada, India and such), signed the Treaty of Versailles. This treaty made the war's end official.

The Treaty mainly provided that Germany:
(1) accept full responsibility for starting the war,
(2) surrender some of its territory to neighboring countries,
(3) give up all of its overseas colonies,
(4) be restricted to a minimal military force, checking the likelihood it could start another war, and
(5) pay reparations to allies, such as France and Belgium that suffered a great deal from the war.

These were harsh impositions on the Germans, and many felt they should not be responsible for what their government had done or for starting the war in the first place. Still, the Treaty's provisions went into effect, not only crippling the German economy but also making the people vulnerable to the rise of a dictatorship.

Just like small towns that suffer widespread unemployment become vulnerable to a local tyrant bent on exerting tight control, Germany fell under the spell of Adolph Hitler and his promises that were doomed to fail.

League of Nations

At the core of the Treaty of Versailles was the agreement of the League of Nations, an international organization of 42 founding members, except the United States. A pacifist president, Woodrow Wilson had tried to keep the U. S. neutral in World War I, but finally, in 1917 he relented and we went to war. A few months later, he introduced his 14-point Peace Program that inspired the formation of the League of Nations in 1919.

Although Wilson wanted the United States to belong to the League, it never joined, because Congress refused, claiming it represented the majority of Americans that no longer wanted to be involved in Europe's international problems.

The League set out to (1) promote disarmament, (2) prevent future world wars, (3) settle international disputes through diplomacy and negotiation and (4) improve the world's welfare.

When all was said and done, the League failed to prevent aggression, and the start of World War II was cold, hard proof of that. Maybe the League just trusted the super powers too much to live up it its expectations.

Another reason we fell into a second global war, in my opinion, goes back to a plentiful supply of World War I generals, who seemed to thrive on war and killing, and who needed conflict to satisfy their lust for power. As someone once said, "An enemy for an army is like a sin for an evangelist." In my opinion, these generals were as dumb as nails.

If you're old enough to remember glass milk bottles, you'll remember how the cream floated to the top. Well, you might think that the generals in the Army are like the cream, always on top. But what happens when the milk goes bad with age? The cream sours and has to be thrown out.

Now, the average cook knows when to throw out bad cream, but the Army kept the cream, their generals, long past their expiration date. The result was that their attitudes and decisions made the lives of the enlisted miserable and brought death and destruction to innocent civilians.

It was as if they lived by a quota: the more dead bodies they could produce, the more medals they could pin to their uniforms. We'll meet up with one of these generals a bit later in our story.

Anyway, thank goodness enough of them finally got sent out to pasture or died, and the likes of Generals Dwight Eisenhower, Courtney Hodges and Omar Bradley were put in command or we would have lost World War II, in my opinion.

And still another cause of World War II was the Great Depression that affected not only the United States, but also much of the rest of the world. I had seen how the Depression affected us at home, but it wasn't until I arrived in England that I realized how far-reaching it was.

World War II

So World War II arrived. Adolph Hitler had snubbed his nose at orders that the German military remain small and non-threatening. In reality, he had managed to build an enormous military power, which at its peak strength grew to more than 10 million men strong with advanced land and air weaponry. And he did it all without most people knowing it.

World War II in Europe began on September 1, 1939 with Hitler's invasion of Poland, a move quickly followed by the British and French declaration of war on Germany. See what I mean by old wounds festering? It didn't take much for others to get into the fray.

The U. S. S. R. invaded eastern Poland and after much resistance, subdued Finland. The battlefields spread to wider arenas in Europe and North Africa, not to mention all the problems arising in the Far East. Between 1939 and 1941, the Germans conquered Poland, Norway, the Netherlands, Belgium, France, Yugoslavia and Greece. By mid-1941, they had overtaken France and Western Europe, but fell short of securing Great Britain.

It seems that Hitler's powerfully equipped army took the British and French by surprise. They had not paid attention to his growing force and, in stark contrast, had let their own armed forces decline, as had the United States. Funds were better spent on domestic programs to help the people.

The Germans scored rather impressive victories early on. Denmark and Norway followed Poland, and in just six weeks the Germans succeeded in driving the British from the continent and forcing France to surrender.

Invading Great Britain was another matter. The German Luftwaffe started bombing London in 1940 to demonstrate air superiority while Hitler formulated plans for a land invasion. Fortunately, crackerjack fighters of the Royal Air Force soundly defeated him.

Set back briefly on that front, the Great Dictator turned toward the Soviet Union. It took almost six months for his armed forces to reach Moscow, and although millions of Russians were captured, bad weather and Russian reinforcements stopped the Germans. On December 11, 1941, Germany declared war on the United States.

British and American air forces counterattacked Germany, beginning in 1942, devastating its great cities. The war soon loomed larger, thanks to a huge buildup of British, French and American troops and military power spreading to North Africa and Italy with the Allied invasions.

In January 1944, General Dwight Eisenhower became the Supreme Allied Commander in Europe. A West Point graduate, Eisenhower was a natural leader. His strong personality, compassion and good nature inspired trust. I had great respect for General Eisenhower and General Bradley, because they cared about the men serving under them and, unlike their predecessors, tried to save lives rather than amass an impressive body count to garner medals.

In February 1944, the heavy bombing raids on London by the Germans were repaid as the US raided Germany's aircraft manufacturing centers. In June the British rained 5,000 tons of bombs on Germany's gun batteries on the Normandy coast to set the stage for the Allied invasion.

Finally, under the great leadership of General Eisenhower came the liberation of France following the brave landings on the beaches of Normandy in June 1944 – Operation Overlord, or D-Day as it became popularly known. It was the largest and most powerful armada to ever set sail.

Later that month, the Germans launched its first V-bomb from Pas-de-Calais, France on Bow, England. It wasn't until autumn of 1944 that the Allies took out the those V-1 launch sites, short-circuiting the Germans ability to bomb England, although they did launch some V-1 and V-2 bombs by air, failing considerably.

Aachen became the first German city to fall to the Allies after they forced the Germans back across the Rhine River.

December brought the bloody Ardennes Offensive, familiarly known as the Battle of the Bulge. By the time the Allies crossed the Rhine and linked up with the Soviets, the Germans were well on their way to defeat.

Eventually the Soviets chased the Germans back to Berlin and bested them on their own turf. Not long after that, on April 30, 1945, Hitler committed suicide. On May 7, 1945, Germany officially surrendered.

Winston Churchill proclaimed May 8, 1945 a national holiday, also known as V-E Day (Victory in Europe). It was a great day for millions of people that had endured bombs and burning cities for the duration of the war.

General Edward Wrenne Timberlake

This seems like an appropriate place to talk about the General that had been groomed to lead the brigade that commanded the 134th AAA Battalion, so here goes.

General Timberlake came from a fine family of West Point graduates, including his father and three brothers. In fact, all three brothers served as generals in World War II.

General Timberlake was outstanding in every way. His personality was outgoing and contagious. Back at West Point, he was known for stirring up the plebes before Army-Navy games, and on the battlefield, he used the same cheerleading strategy to get his men all fired up.

The 49th AAA Brigade was activated at Fort Davis, North Carolina. This became the first unit that General Timberlake would lead into combat after he assumed command of the 49ers in June 1943 and got his stars.

He led the 49ers to England in November 1943 and took over control of the Blandford AAA Training Camp where his artillerymen trained both American and British troops for the forthcoming invasion of Europe.

As part of the First Army's antiaircraft cover, the 49th Brigade stormed ashore on June 6, 1944 on Omaha Beach and played an aggressive role in First Army's march to Paris in August.

All right, so now we know that the war is going on and we know that we have a great General ready to lead us into battle. Now it is time to find out just what the 134th AAA Battalion was and what part we were destined to play in World War II.

The Gunners of Battery D
[I'm in the second row, far left]
134th AAA Battalion

Chapter 3

134th AAA Battalion

Diplomats are just as essential
to starting a war as
soldiers are for finishing it.
Will Rogers
1879-1935

The 134th Anti-Aircraft Artillery (AAA) Gun Battalion, organized into five Batteries (A, B, C, D and Headquarters), was activated on June 10, 1943 at the Great Lakes Training Center in Chicago. That's almost exactly the same time that General Timberlake was storming ashore Omaha Beach.

For the most part, the 134th was made up of young men, who had never fought in combat or set foot on foreign soil. We were part of a growing army that was an equal opportunity employer: rich and poor alike served in the Big War. Although we had completed basic training, we were still green and clueless about what we were really going to face. Of course, we had no idea of our final destination or the part we would play in helping to defeat Hitler's Nazi army.

I was one of almost 700 men serving in the 134th, and I was a gunner in Battery D, although not all men in D were gunners. Others, like John Pfeister, had equally important jobs, like making sure our trucks were where they were supposed to be and Earl Gamble, who treated the sick and wounded, although not being with an infantry battalion, our medics encountered few serious battle wounds.

Captain Lawrence Foley, a native of Fall River, Massachusetts, was the commander of Battery D, and, as the chain of command went, he reported to the commander of the 134th AAA Battalion, who reported to General Edward Timberlake. Second in command of the Battalion were 1st Lt. John Lenaeus, 1st Lt. Donald R. Kummer and 1st Lt. Robert A. Young, whom I recall was a very kind man.

Throughout the war, the command of the 134th changed quite frequently for one reason or another. One could speculate why, but I surmise it was because some of the commanders fell short of the required leadership skills and were sent packing.

We were in Chicago just a short time; then we were transferred to Fort Bliss, Texas to train in the desert. Lord, how I loved Fort Bliss!

I latched onto a cute little Mexican girl, who worked at a bar outside of El Paso. The owner and his wife took a liking to me, and I had my share of free meals there. The only problem was that they did not like me with the Mexican cutie, so I had to choose. I left both of them, as we got orders to move out.

Camp Livingston, Louisiana was our next destination, and it was like going from the frying pan into the fire. The temperature and humidity stayed around 98 percent the whole time we were there, which thankfully was not very long. It was here that I celebrated my 20th birthday, just five years after leaving home as a southern Indiana hayseed.

Before daylight of June 24, 1944, we rose, loaded our personal baggage and boarded the train that would take us through the Midwest and East, finally arriving at Camp Miles Standish, Massachusetts two days later. What wonderful weather after sweating it out in Louisiana!

For the next six days we received shots, watched training films, attended lectures and became accustomed to barking orders, lugging our duffel bags and operating in darkness, which would save our lives later.

On July 2, they boarded a train for Boston. We still did not know our final destination. We ate box lunches aboard the train, as it meandered along the harbor and stopped at the pier. After we detrained, we were lined up on the pier.

American Red Cross girls passed out donuts and orange juice but by then no one was hungry. We just wanted to know where we were going! Some gambled that it was just going to be a dry run.

To the marching tunes of a local band, up the gangplank we went, soon settling in on the U. S. S. Brazil. The following day, we set sail from Boston harbor and watched as the last images of the USA faded from view.

Soon after we set sail, we were given instructions on the use of our Mae West life jackets and what to do in a lifeboat drill. We followed this same routine for a few minutes each day we were at sea.

July 4, 1944 came and went without fireworks, but some of the men enjoyed serious crap games to help pass the time at sea. On July 12, we docked in Gourock, Renfrew, Scotland. My God, how beautiful! I stood on deck of the Brazil, drinking in the scenery. The sea was calm and the sun was just coming up behind the city. Although we had set sail with about 50 ships, we were the only one of our convoy at anchor.

Of course, we were eager to go ashore, but we had to stay on ship that night. The launches picked us up the next morning and took us ashore. I was impressed by the harbor, because I had always read how dirty and overrun with rats harbors were. Well, this harbor was clean.

Excitement was at a very high pitch. Immediately, we boarded a waiting train that was small and quaint by American standards. Scottish Red Cross girls served coffee and donuts onboard.

Next stop: Camp Blackshaw Moor, near Leek in Staffordshire, England. We were there from July 13 to August 1. Although it was raining when we arrived, our spirits remained high, in part because we had their first mail call since setting sail from Boston. And the English girls were so beautiful and sweet. Some of us did not take long to become acquainted!

For the next few days, we got our trucks and 90mm ammo and picked up our radar equipment. The rest of the time was spent getting ready for combat.

On August 1, we proceeded by motor convoy more than 140 miles to Camp Yaddington. As we drove across England, I continued to drink in the beauty of its countryside…the green rolling hills…quaint, picturesque hamlets…and her famous fog. That's when I started my love affair with England that lingers to this day! I fully expected to see Robin Hood and his merry men ride up any minute.

Soon, I could see how the Depression had hit England, just as it had devastated lives at home. People were poorly dressed, and almost everyone walked, as there was a scarcity of cars or, at least, petrol (gasoline).

As we neared London, we experienced our first reality of war – air raid sirens screaming and bombs buzzing overhead. Believe it or not, we were all quite eager to see our first V-1 or buzz bomb, as our advance party had described it to us. The British referred to these flying bombs as divers or Doodlebugs.

The V-1, developed by the German Luftwaffe, was a guided, pilot-less missile that carried a one-ton warhead. The launch site was a stationary ramp, and the traveled 400-410 mph at an altitude of 4,000 feet and a range of 150 miles.

Germany launched this amazing new weapon from Pas-de-Calais on the northern coast of France in June 1944. Before it was all over, they had fired 9,520 V-1 bombs on southern England, and 4,621 were destroyed by anti-aircraft fire or British fighters. The bombs were devastating to the cities of London and Antwerp, Belgium, in all killing 6,184 people.

Our new position, which would become known as Shrapnel Heights, was at Hythe in beautiful Kent County, England. On August 2, we moved onto the golf course located on the West Side of Folkstone, England, which is on the English Channel near Dover. We referred to it as Buzz Bomb Alley.

Our job was to shoot and destroy the V-1 bombs that were playing hell on London. The British couldn't hit a bull in the ass with a handful of gravel, but with our new equipment, we were getting a high percentage.

Dug into the Cliffs of Dover, the British – who invented radar – had a great system in place, which was connected to our completely automatic radar. Operating the British radar were 5000 young women, known as Wrens. They were great and always on target.

When they picked up a target, the data was sent to my computer. It was my duty to alert the guns of this information. As a result, the four 90mm guns locked on the target, with fuses cut, and guns loaded waiting on the gunnery officer to order "Commence fire!" This was all done very quickly, considering the speed of the bomb. The gun crews were very, very efficient.

August 5, 1944 marked the turning point of the war or so we would like to think. That's when Battery D went into action. When the WREN girl sounded "Folkestone Harbor Diver Alarm", the commander automatically gave the order to commence fire, and we were in action.

All the time the Germans were sending over the daily ration of divers and with our poor equipment, we were filling the air with flack and hitting nothing. The M-7 director [computer] that I was operating was absolutely terrible; then in short order, the M-9 came, and we started knocking the hell out of those divers.

Our only problem was that the M-9 could compute only up to the miles per hour that the diver traveled, so we had to make contact with it over the English Channel. If we let the diver pass our fire over the Channel, it went on to London.

Eventually the more efficient M-10 director replaced by the M-9, and we scored even more hits. Thanks to the Wrens and our excellent shooting, we reduced to only 20 percent the bombs that reached England by August.

On August 30th Battery D shut down operations for 24 hours and everyone took off on pass. Several of the guys went to London, Canterbury, Dover and all points between. Once we established how deadly accurate our firepower was, each battery was allowed to cease operations for one day each week. Even with one battery off duty, few bombs got through.

We always had a guard to spot any of the V-bombs that were falling in our area. Over the radio came an alert. I looked out the window of the M-10 director I was operating, only to see a bomb coming straight at me at 400 mph! It ticked the top of the M-10, slid onto the wet grass and came to a halt on the golf course. It was not damaged at all.

[Many years later, I visited Greencastle, Indiana and there on a pedestal was a V-bomb! DePauw University was located nearby, and in the library there I did some research and learned that the bomb in Greencastle was the same one that almost hit me in England!]

Although the gunners in Battery D were losing sleep over buzz bombs, most of our lack of sleep could be attributed to activities of a sweeter kind. As we soon discovered, the English girls were eager, entertaining and friendly. In short, there was a lot of fraternizing going on with American GIs.

The problem was there was just no place to go, other than the beach, where all the areas were heavily mined in case the Germans invaded. This meant we suddenly had to become mine experts or be blown sky high, so those of us that broke the law and used this area, walked gently and of course made love gently. I can report there were no explosions of the mines, but plenty of other types!

It was strange but the girls in England and later in Europe did not fear getting pregnant. In fact, they seemed to welcome it. One must remember there was an acute shortage of available men during the war, which, of course, was next to heaven for young American GIs, many of whom had never been with a woman.

One night in the Folkestone area, a girl and I were necking with her back against a large tree. This was, of course, during a total blackout, which meant I might have been with the ugliest girl in town. All of a sudden, there was a flash, then one hell of an explosion. The tree trunk saved us, as an 18-inch shell hit a building behind us.

There was a fine hotel – the Majestic – in Folkestone, where I took a cute little Wren to dinner. We drew some stares from the people dining there, but that didn't spoil our enjoyment of the place. We dined and danced the night away.

The Majestic became my favorite haunt whenever I had a night off. In fact, I went there so many times the orchestra would strike up the American patrol song. It embarrassed me, so I requested that they stop. I loved the class of people that frequented the hotel and enjoyed the great food, which was rare in those days in England.

The next time we ceased operations for a 24-hour pass was September 7, 1944. A battery party was scheduled that night at Leas Cliff Hall, but the German channel guns started shelling the coast and the Hall didn't open. The refreshments, including the girls, were taken out to the battery position and the party was held in the house and the surrounding area.

A musical magician

There is a lot more to tell about the activities of the 134th AAA Battalion, but first we need to catch up on an American phenomenon, a musical magician that landed in England just a short time after we arrived.

Even before he arrived, Glenn Miller, born Alton Glen Miller, was weaving his musical notes into the hearts of soldiers everywhere. He had enlisted and brought his band to England to demonstrate closer ties to the war effort.

Let's look at where he started and what led to his amazing rise to fame at a time when music, which ordinarily one might not associate with war, became the salve that sowed broken hearts and the balm that eased the pain of widespread death and destruction.

Chapter 4

Alton Glen Miller

If a man does not keep pace with his companions,
perhaps it is because he hears a different drummer.
Let him step to the music, which he hears,
however measured or faraway.
Henry David Thoreau
1817 - 1862

During World War II, radio was king, and whoever captured the airwaves won the hearts of men and women around the world. Glenn Miller was one who did, and his music soothed the souls of weary soldiers and provided the backdrop to love and romance far away from home.

Despite Colonel Theodore Banks' remark, "You aren't going to win the war with piccolos", music proved as vital as warm coats for the daily struggles on the front lines. The diversity of musical styles – from marches to blues – fed the souls of troops of all stripes and colors.

As the war gained momentum, Glenn Miller, whose band had been gaining popularity in the United States, decided to join the military and do his part overseas. After dissolving his civilian band in September 1942, he set out to entertain the troops for the war effort, initially landing assignments on the east coast with his Army Air Force Technical Training Corps Band.

Juggling popular engagements at Yale University, a regular radio broadcast, called "I Sustain the Wings" – at first out of Boston and later from New York – and war bond drives as far west as St. Louis, Miller's band delighted dancehall crowds and at-home listeners alike.

Who was this maestro that touched the hearts of millions?

Early life

The folks of rural Clarinda in southwestern Iowa had no idea what was given to them on March 1, 1904, when Alton Glen (later changed to Glenn) was born to Elmer and Mattie Lou Miller. He would certainly put this little town on the map!

The family eventually sought greener pastures, moving to Tryon, Nebraska in 1907. Glenn's mother played a simple pump organ to ease their lonely times there. When Elmer's father brought home a mandolin, he may have had no idea how it would affect young Glenn. It didn't take Glenn long to trade it in for a used horn, which he practiced day and night.

His mother started a school, and her children sang songs as they rode in a wagon on their way to school. Glenn appreciated music and recognized early on the impact it had on people.

In 1915, the family moved to Grant City, Missouri where Glenn attended grade school and worked for the town bands man. He received his first trombone and played in the local band. As the saying goes, the rest was history.

In 1918, Glenn's family moved to Fort Morgan, Colorado, where Glenn attended high school. During his senior year, he tried out for football and was chosen by the Colorado High School Sports Association as "the best left end in Colorado."

Football didn't capture Glenn's interest, as he was becoming very attracted to the sound of the new dance band music. He enjoyed it so much that he and some of his classmates formed their own band.

Instead of attending his high school graduation in 1921, he went to Laramie, Wyoming to play in a band. His mother accepted his diploma.

By now, Glenn had decided that he would be a professional musician. His first contract was signed with a Dixieland band called Senter's Sentapeeds.

Another opportunity came that enabled him to play in the Holly Moyer Orchestra in Boulder and earn enough money to attend the University of Colorado. He spent most of his time away from school, however, attending auditions and playing any gigs he could get. Glenn dropped out of college and decided to concentrate on becoming a professional musician.

Early career

Fueling that ambition was a job with the Tommy Watkins Orchestra in 1924. He later studied with Joseph Schillinger, whom Miller credited with helping him create his own special "sound". While he was with Schillinger, he composed *Moonlight Serenade,* the most recognizable of his songs.

He went to Los Angeles to tap band opportunities there. He soon joined the Ben Pollack Orchestra, and while there, he roomed with clarinetist Benny Goodman, another rising star.

In 1928, while working in Los Angeles and Chicago, Glenn moved to New York City, where he worked with the bands of Ben Pollack, Red Nichols and Paul Ash as a trombonist and arranger. The latter apparently was his first love. That year, he married Helen Burger, his college sweetheart.

During the 1930s, Miller earned a living working as a freelance trombonist with different bands and compiling musical arrangements. Beginning in 1932, he organized a few notable bands, including the Smith Ballew Band for whom he worked two years as its manager, arranger and trombonist, the Dorsey brothers' first full-time Big Band and Ray Noble's American Band.

First band

Glenn's first band didn't become a reality until 1937; however, financial constraints caused the band to break up. That's difficult to imagine, when you consider they recorded such all-time hits as *Peg O' My Heart, Anytime, Any Day, Anywhere, Moonlight Bay, I'm Sitting on Top of the World, I Got Rhythm, Sleepy Time Gal, Time on My Hands,* among others.

Discouraged, he returned to New York, where he dedicated himself to finding his own unique sound. "A band ought to have a sound all of its own. It ought to have a personality," he once said.

He finally decided to make the clarinet play a melodic line with a tenor saxophone on the same note, while three saxophones harmonized. That was the sound he was looking for! "[The saxophone sound] was always intended to be an all-around combination, but when we do play a swing number, we expect and try to make it swing as much as possible," he once remarked.

Second band

Formed in March 1938, the second Glenn Miller Orchestra broke attendance records up and down the East Coast. His new style, the new Miller "sound" paid off and the band outsold other bands throughout the country. At the New York State Fair in Syracuse, it attracted the largest dancing crowd in the city's history. The next night, it topped Guy Lombardo's all-time record at the Hershey Park Ballroom in Pennsylvania.

The Orchestra was invited to perform at Carnegie Hall with three of the greatest bands ever, including Benny Goodman, where he won critical acclaim for carving out a style that set him apart from other bands of the day.

In 1939, Miller's band attracted a nationwide following as they played important gigs on the East Coast. Tied to those performances were radio broadcasts that heightened his appeal across the country. Early 1940 brought Miller an announcement by Down Beat Magazine that his band had topped all other bands in its Sweet Band Poll. Miller also started his Moonlight Serenade radio series for Chesterfield cigarettes.

Despite his success and perhaps because of his self-effacing personality, Miller claimed, "I haven't [got] a great jazz band and I don't want one. A dozen colored bands have a beat better than mine."

Miller was in constant demand for recording sessions and movie making. Two films – "Sun Valley Serenade" (1941), which introduced *Chattanooga Choo Choo.* His band appeared in "Orchestra Wives" in 1942. On the February 10, 1942 Chesterfield radio broadcast, RCA presented Miller the first gold record ever awarded, honoring the 1,200,000[th] sale of *Chattanooga Choo Choo.*

Other popular Miller hits of the day were *A String of Pearls* and *Pennsylvania 6-5000,* which was the real telephone number of the Hotel Pennsylvania, later known as the Statler Hotel, in Manhattan.

One music critic – The New York Times – wrote in January 1940, "[Glenn Miller's] arrangements are inventive and refreshing. He never forgets the melodic line. He lets you recognize the tune."

Just as Miller was hitting the high notes at home, the war grew larger abroad and started to take its toll on many of the big bands, as musicians and the rest of the young men in America received their draft notices.

Glenn Miller would look at the war from his own perspective and determine how he could help the war effort. We next look at how he managed to do that.

Chapter 5

Major Glenn Miller

We didn't come here to set any fashions
in music. We merely came to bring a
much needed touch of home to some lads,
who have been here a couple of years.
Major Glenn Miller
In a letter from England
Summer 1944

If you lived through World War II – whether or not you were in the service – can you honestly listen to Glenn Miller's *Moonlight Serenade* today without getting goose bumps or having the tears well up? His "sound" provided the musical backdrop to the war effort worldwide and eventual news of his deployment to England sent hearts fluttering in the young men and women, who found love and romance amid a bombardment of buzz bombs.

In 1942, Miller was at the peak of his civilian career, but he thought he could serve the war effort better by joining the service. He was too old to be drafted, so he volunteered for the Navy, but was told his services were not needed there.

Then, he wrote to Army Brigadier General Charles Young, whom he persuaded to accept him so that he could "put a little more spring into the feet of our marching men and a little more joy in their hearts and to be placed in charge of a modernized army band."

After being accepted, Miller's civilian band performed its last concert on September 27, 1942. The event was such a tearjerker that the band couldn't finish playing its theme song *Moonlight Serenade.*

Captain Miller

As part of the Army Specialist Corps, Captain Glenn Miller also enjoyed the rank of Director of Bands. He formed a large marching band that would serve as the core of service orchestras. This is when he first met resistance from the old military guard. His modern version of military music did not play well with those generals.

To further his own kind of music, Miller formed an orchestra consisting of a 24-piece dance band with 21 string players chosen from a number of symphony orchestras. Over the next 18 months, he arranged music and created and directed his own 50-member band, for which he chose servicemen who had belonged to the best bands in the United States. He based the 418th Army Air Force Band at Yale University on March 20, 1943. Their post duties included reveille, taps, march, retreat and entertainment.

Captain Miller's mission was morale building, bringing a touch of home to the troops and modernizing military music. In his spare time, he raised millions of dollars in war bond drives.

In 1944, the long-awaited allied invasion of Europe was in an advanced stage of preparation. General Eisenhower was acutely aware of the need to sustain the morale of the thousands of American servicemen and women gathering in southern England. To that end, the British Broadcasting Company [BBC] to set up a new radio service, "The Allied Expeditionary Forces [AEF] Programme", featuring the U. S. Army Air Force Band.

Back in the states, Miller attracted Air Corps recruits through his "I Sustain the Wings" weekly radio broadcasts. The day after D-Day, the invasion of Normandy beaches, Miller received permission to take his band overseas. To open "Wings" on June 10, 1944, Captain Glenn Miller reported, "It's been a big week for our side. Over on the beaches of Normandy, our boys have fired the opening guns of the long awaited drive to liberate the world."

On June 28, 1944 – just days after the 134th AAA Battalion docked in Scotland – Miller and his AEF band arrived in Glasgow aboard the Queen Elizabeth. After a brief stay at 25 Sloane Street in London, where there was a constant barrage of buzz bombs, Miller decided to move the band to a safer location.

On July 2, he and the band moved to new quarters at Twinwood Airfield in Bedford, Bedfordshire. Twinwood was not an American bomber base, but the AEF Band used it to give concerts throughout the country. The day after the band settled there, a buzz bomb landed in front of their old quarters in London, destroying the building and killing 100 people.

On July 9, the band made its first "live" broadcast. Their music became extremely popular not only with the American servicemen, but also with millions of Britons tuning in their radio broadcasts.

Miller defined wartime music; in short, his popular music reached an all-time high and was devoured by the troops in England, on the continent and around the world. While in England, the Glenn Miller band gave more than 800 performances to an estimated one million Allied servicemen and women. In just one month, Miller wrote home, his Army Air Force Band played at 35 different bases, while performing 40 radio broadcasts in their spare time.

You had to have been there to know how much Miller's music captivated your soul. We took every opportunity to hear his music and dance to our favorite tunes. When we were unable to do either, we let the music play in our minds.

Miller's popularity, to be sure, soon eclipsed the popularity of the traditional military brass of the 8th Army Air Force. I firmly believe that some General, who hated Miller's music, became jealous. Miller would not acquiesce to his demands that he play marching music to keep the troops mindful of their military mission; he persevered instead in furthering the dance music that the men and women so loved.

Put yourself in the General's place. Let's assume you were in total command of an air base and you're in love with John Philips Sousa's marching music. Without your permission, someone sends the Rolling Stones and orders you to keep the band on your base. How long do you think you would tolerate that distraction to firing up your troops? How long do you think you would be able to hear that music day in and day out before scheming to get rid of it?

As a matter of fact, rumors were flying that Miller was about to be sent home, most likely because he refused to play that oom-pah-pah music that the old generals wanted him to play. Being discharged and sent home would have ended Miller's career as an entertainer, and he knew it. He wanted to avoid that at all costs.

What were Miller's alternatives? In the process of solving that problem, would he unwittingly orchestrate his own demise?

Chapter 6

September 9, 1944

There are two sides to every story,
then there's what really happened.
Mike Rivero
www.whatreallyhappened.com

What was Glenn Miller to do? Surely, he hated his superior officers for insisting that he play their kind of music instead of the sound that had taken England by storm. He must have gotten wind that they were cutting papers to return him to the United States.

His superior officers left this dirty deed to his commanding officer. They used him as a scapegoat. This is why no word of the plan to return Miller to the States became known to anybody, because heads would have rolled.

Surely his thoughts must have run along these lines, 'I must get out of this command!' The only option was to go to Paris, where he could get a new command with brass that appreciated his style and not those old generals that preferred marching music while getting drunk at the Officers Club.

While waiting for the right opportunity to go to Paris, Miller and his band continued to play their popular tunes. I'm sure many former GIs remember, as I do, when we were just over our heads in love and Glenn Miller's music had a lot to do with our feelings. All the girls were sweet and friendly. It's no wonder he and his music are still so popular. I'm not ashamed to admit I still cloud up when I hear it.

September 1944

The gunners of Battery D were positioned in Folkestone, having succeeded in curtailing much of the V-1 bombing. I was operating the M-10 computer director, which was hooked up with the radar operated by the English Wrens.

In early September, however, the Germans sent over wave after wave of bombs. Then all of a sudden, it became deathly quiet. The next day was the same. No bombs flying overhead. The Morning Reports, submitted daily by Captain Foley, substantiate these facts.

During the bombing lull, another GI and I decided to walk through the fields to see Canterbury Cathedral. We were nearing the church and before us was a tavern in an open field, which was not unusual. Suddenly, an 18-inch shell, fired by the Germans from France, hit the tavern. It was just a lucky hit; nevertheless, there was nothing left. It was reduced to bricks and trash. It was strange, because both of us simply turned around at the same time and returned to our outfit without saying a word.

If you've ever been to England, you know you can expect two things for sure – fog in various degrees of density and a misty kind of rain. On rare occasions, you wake up to a clear, sunny day. Perhaps it's because they are rare that you remember when they occur, especially if such a day coincides with something significant.

I couldn't tell you specifically what the weather was like any other day that I was in England, but I vividly remember that the morning of September 9, 1944 was clear and bright, the start of a beautiful English day. I was stationed at my M-10 director, wondering if the bombing lull would break.

Early that afternoon, Major Glenn Miller and his pilot most likely took off in a single-engine plane from Twinwood Airfield 50 miles north of London. They were headed for Paris. Miller had a reason for going there, and so did his pilot, who was about to be court martialed on black market charges. Records indicate a third party was with them on this flight.

The plane was small – some say a Piper Cub – and stripped down. There were probably no life preservers on board, due to lack of space from all that black market loot that had eager buyers in Paris waiting for it. The flight plan did not allow them to fly over London, which was absolutely forbidden. They took off on one of the best weather days we had while I was stationed in England. And there were no V-1 bombs or other planes in the area.

Suddenly my director came alive. Dover had picked up a target coming from the northwest and when no IFF (Identification Friend or Foe) signal came forth, Dover assumed the plane was an enemy target.

"Folkestone Harbor Diver Alarm!"

Immediately the information I received in my director passed to the gunners on the coast of England. They turned their guns from their normal easterly direction to the north.

I also requested an IFF response from the target. No return signal was given. I sent another signal, no response. In fact, I sent out four IFF signals, when normally I would have to ask only once; the IFF response was automatic.

I reported this information to Captain Foley. I also informed him that it appeared the target was not an enemy plane, as it was flying at a low altitude, at slow air speed and was coming from the northwest, heading toward France. I also noted the craft had no IFF.

No sooner were these words out of my mouth than I heard "Commence fire!" Thirty-six rounds were fired after which Dover gave the "Target down" report. I knew we had killed whoever was in that small plane, shot down between Ramsgate and Dover over the North Sea.

There was no way the guns could have stopped. They had cut the fuses and had to fire the guns, as the fuses could not be retracted. We hit Miller's plane on the first four rounds, totally obliterating it and rendering everything to dust.

Sure enough, the AFN (Armed Forces Network) radio airwaves carried the report that Glenn Miller was missing over the Channel.

To this day, I cannot understand how the AFN was allowed to put what they did on the air, although the 8th Air Force did not have complete control over the radio. I mean, discussing Major Miller was a purely hostile act towards the high command. This makes me believe that someone knew a lot more than they could say, but managed to broadcast part of the truth.

When I went off duty later I passed by the command post, as the Captain walked out.

"Captain, we killed Glenn Miller," I said.

The Captain's face was pale, which was not his natural hue, being a good Irishman, who made regular use of his officer's monthly whiskey allotment. He was fully aware of what we had done.

"Shut your goddamn mouth," he ordered sternly.

Later that day, he surprised me when he ordered, "This stays between us."

I said, "Okay."

Throughout the remainder of the war, Captain Foley rarely spoke another word to me or looked in my direction. We had entered into a conspiracy of silence, and there was nothing else to say.

Now, how was the Captain going to keep this between just the two of us? He had shot off 36 rounds of 90mm ammunition.

The next day – September 10 – he covered this horrible deed in his morning report, stating that he was calibrating his guns from 1400 hours (2:00 p.m.) to 1420 (2:20 p.m.) the day before. Here are his words exactly as they appeared in the morning report of September 10, 1944:

RECORD OF EVENTS
FIRED 32 RDS FOR CALIBRATION
FR. 1400 TO 1420

So did we or did we not shoot down Miller's plane? The morning report proves that we did, because the timing was perfect! The report got the Captain off the hook, too.

Now, the next day The Stars and Stripes, the daily newspaper of the U. S. Armed Forces, carried nothing about Miller being missing. There is good reason to explain that, other than the fact that the paper routinely did not carry obituaries. The 8th Air Force controlled it. Every bit of news had to pass through the Army censors before it went public (to the troops). That meant that the 8th Air Force was not about to release any news that would implicate them in Miller's disappearance.

To further my feelings of his missing, let's assume a very important person was reported missing on a short flight. Does anybody think nothing would be in the papers?

One had to live in those times when troop morale had a tremendous effect on the outcome of the war, and Glenn Miller's music had this powerful impact. If the news had come out that this Piper Cub with no instruments was given the green light to fly as a target across 15 miles of guns, the troop morale would have gone down as fast as Miller's plane disintegrated.

8th Air Force complicity

We did the Air Force a favor, if you want to think of it that way. I firmly believe some General, who hated Miller for his music, was behind all of this. I believe I am 100 percent correct in knowing how the brass operated. They killed Glenn Miller, maybe not deliberately but it seems that way.

The General was upset because Miller switched from marching music to his popular tunes of love and romance. Even when ordered to discontinue that kind of music, Miller continued to play at parties and clubs all over England. The General knew that sending Miller up in a plane without IFF would make it impossible for him to get by the 15 miles of trigger-happy guns lining the coast. What better way to get rid of that distraction to the war?

In my opinion, the 8th Air Force was at fault for allowing Major Miller to fly in an ill-equipped plane. Common sense should have been used when allowing such an important person to fly in such a plane. Let me tell you; Major Miller was important to all of the GIs in England and, for that matter, the whole world!

If someone could dig up the commanding officer of Miller's detachment at that time, you would find a bastard who had complete command over a bunch of officers with absolutely no guts who kissed his ass every morning and evening. I saw these sons-of-bitches. I pity Glenn Miller for his bad experience with them or, I should say, one of them.

This is my opinion. Nobody will ever convince me the 8th Air Force didn't have his plane on radar. They had to know when we shot his Piper Cub down.

The problem was that the radar operators had been so busy with thousands of planes on their screens that one more downed aircraft would hardly be noticed. You had to see to believe all the targets and friendly aircraft that showed up on their screens. But the 8th Air Force knew when Miller took off and when he went down.

Our battalion was the only one that fired that day. The British and Americans had guns dug in from above Dover down 15 miles along the coast. If the big brass had had an interest in Miller's disappearance, they could have solved the puzzle in mere minutes, but they had no interest in learning the truth.

Again, this is why the true Glenn Miller story has never been revealed. Whoever issued that plane to a black market dealer flying in front of 15 miles of trigger-happy young AA (Anti Aircraft) guns eager to down any plane that did not return the IFF signal knew Miller didn't have a chance. In contrast: Look at the protection given to USO entertainers. Have you ever heard of one of their planes getting lost or going down?

8th Air Force cover-up

The 8th Air Force was compelled to cover up Miller's disappearance and death, as troop morale would have taken a mighty blow had the truth come out.

Now, how to cover it all up. This act has been going on for 62 years! The best part of the whole deal is that no one blames the 8th Air Force. They just simply sit back and read the drunken fabrications from people who really have no idea what happened but are lucky enough to get their 15 minutes of fame for spreading these wild stories. All the while, the guilty parties are sitting back with their guilty consciences and enjoying their Scotch and soda.

Perpetuating a lie or cover-up of this magnitude takes a concerted effort on the part of a great many people. It's a communications scheme, requiring considerable pre-planning that starts *before* the incident occurs; otherwise, leaks could occur and all sorts of snafus arise that cannot be controlled. The Air Force *controlled* the information about Miller's demise – except for the one broadcast aired on AFN the day of his disappearance [and death].

First of all, the Army censored every letter a GI mailed home. After all, we were fighting a very intelligent enemy that had many spies at work. The AFN disc jockeys never let up about Glenn Miller's disappearance, as well as some juicy gossip about him, including shacking up with a girl in Paris. I heard these stories in England, while working 12 hours a day at my M-10 director, which had a radio.

See, I had to have heard all this on AFN in England, because not long after we shot down Miller's plane, our battalion was shipped off to France, where we had no need for the power plant for my radio. Our action was 100 percent ground activity. The M-10 and radar (and radio) were never used again until we sat down in Liège in November 1944.

Why weren't those AFN broadcasts recorded or, if they were, where are they now? Their mysterious disappearance further convinces me that there was a cover-up in motion. The people behind this dirty deed had the power and the tools to make it "go away." I must say they did a good job.

That the United States Air Force has covered up what really happened to Glenn Miller should come as no surprise to any student of military history. Military and intelligence officers – not just of the United States – have kept from public view certain facts and strategies to perpetuate their own agendas.

43

Years and years later, the lies slowly unravel and the truth takes shape. Just like we are doing now.

Here are just three examples of U. S. military/CIA cover-up stories:

Klaus Barbie

On July 17, 1983, The New York Times published an article by Ralph Blumenthal, citing that high United States Army intelligence officers paid and shielded Klaus Barbie as an informant for years after World War II. This was done "despite their knowledge that the former Gestapo officer was wanted in France for war crimes." According to some of the former agents, "the Americans also used Mr. Barbie to gather information on the French. One reason, they said, that American officials refused to turn over Mr. Barbie to the French, who were searching for him, was fear of what the former Gestapo officer could tell the French about American counterintelligence operations, including those directed against French communists."

As an earlier editorial in The New York Times of March 3, 1983 stated, "Is it really to much to ask the United States to admit or deny having shielded one of Germany's notorious war criminals from postwar justice in France?" The editorial posed the question because the Nazi hunters that tracked Barbie to Bolivia charge that American forces arrested the "Butcher of Lyons" but released him after paying him for intelligence about the Soviet zone of occupied Germany.

A former U. S. Army intelligence agent substantiated some of the charges, as he said he paid and supervised Barbie until 1948. As of that date – in 1983 – the State Department, CIA and Pentagon have been "looking into" the matter and the Justice Department claims to know nothing about it. Right.

Adolf Eichmann

In another wartime secret exposed, in 2006, an Associated Press article revealed that the CIA covered up Nazi war crimes and the whereabouts of Adolf Eichmann.

General George Patton

And, most recently, the cause of death of General Patton has come under closer scrutiny. Stories are popping up all over the place about how and where the General died. Well, a good friend of mine in Germany was a motorcycle MP patrolling the Autobahn and was the first to come upon an accident. The accident involved a United States command car that had crashed into a 2½-ton U. S. Army truck. When my friend approached the command car, he looked into the back seat and there he saw General Patton, dead as a doornail.

If all of these events surrounding World War II figures could be covered up for many years, it stands to reason that the true story about the death of Glenn Miller could easily be covered up, as well.

90-day wait

It is common knowledge in the military that if a GI goes missing, is captured or deserts, a 90-day period must elapse before the military declares the GI missing or dead. His outfit gives him 90 days to show up; if not, some time after 90 days, he is declared dead officially. In some cases, the wait was as long as six months.

In one such incident, our mess sergeant, a proud Irishman, went on furlough to Ireland for two weeks and stayed for just shy of six months. He got married while he was in Ireland. He was not listed as AWOL all the time he was gone. He returned just before the six-month deadline and just went back to work in the kitchen, like nothing happened.

The 8th Air Force would not have notified Miller's wife immediately upon knowing he was missing. What if, as the rumors flew, he had gone to Paris to lay up with a woman there for a few weeks? To report him missing would have upset his family, who might have assumed him dead. Well, in this case, he was.

So, what's the 8th Air Force to do? They had to come up with a new date for his death. If the Army declared him dead (or permanently missing) on December 15th, that meant automatically that he first went missing at least 90 days before that, according to the way the military handled missing GIs in World War II.

The 8th Air Force adjutant that set the 15th as the official date of Miller's death was doing his job, just as our outfit did its job when we fired on a plane with no IFF signal.

The word "official" is the key to this cover up. What it means is that the search is over and the books are closed. Let us assume the rumors were correct and Miller was shacked up in France, and they both tired of each other and he came wandering back into camp.

To show you how the 8th Air Force manipulated the news to further its cover-up, the December 27, 1944 issue of The Stars and Stripes carried a small article: Glenn Miller Is Missing On Hop From U. K. to Paris. The article states Miller as officially "missing in action" since December 15th.

In another story, the 8th Air Force, which, as we see, had declared Miller missing on December 15th had him officially declared dead on the 20th! Yet another report noted that the Air Force officially informed Miller's wife on Christmas Eve! There is no way the Army would ever declare a member dead in five days – or nine days – of the day he went missing!

This confirms that we shot him down on September 9th. Without confirmation, such as the "official notification" of December 15th, I really felt readers would put me in the same class as other GIs and media, who came up with all their stories about what really happened to Miller.

The whole cover-up seems to have been thought up by the dumbest people on the base, yet the pitiful part is that they got by with it all these years.

A foggy theory

The most glaring error in the 8th Air Force's selection of the official date of Miller's missing status is that on December 15, 1944, all of southeastern England was socked in by such dense fog that no planes were allowed to take off, except radar-controlled military planes. Not even the buses in London were running!

The story that Miller's little plane took off in blinding fog is utterly preposterous! Hell, all of Europe was blanketed with the same fog! What air controller would allow such a plane – without instruments – to take off when the pilot couldn't even see the runway?

Single-engine planes were used for training and as artillery spotters during a battle. They just were not equipped with instruments for that type of trip!

No one thought to check the weather reports for December 15th, yet that is the date that has been used by conspiracy theorists and the media ever since. What a shame!

Time for an official inquiry

Why have I waited these many years to come forth with this story? Because I made a promise, and I kept it.

It is time for the truth to be told. Just as I believe I have an obligation to history to tell the truth about what really happened to Glenn Miller, so does the 8th Air Force to confess cover-ups that have warped history for many years.

In all the speculation about what happened to Glenn Miller, I have heard only a couple of times that maybe his plane was shot down – one report even stated it was shot down by friendly fire. I can tell you for certain that no inquiries were ever made of Battery D that shot him down.

The After Action reports, written by the commanding officer each month for the previous month's activities of the 134th AAA Battalion and batteries, reveal exactly what I remember about September 1944. There were no incoming German bombs from September 9th to the 13th. Enemy coastal guns in France began bombarding the English coast again on September 14th.

In all this time, I have never read or heard of any questions being asked by the powers-that-be. This gives you an idea how powerful the Army was during the war. If it didn't suit them, they shut it up!

If ever there is an inquiry concerning Glenn Miller's disappearance – if it is done properly – many of these bastards will be charged posthumously. If a person really studies this Glenn Miller story, it is so out in the open that they wanted him dead. The problem is that those that know the truth are afraid to come forward for fear of being blackballed by the other officers.

I challenge anyone to prove me wrong. Not one officer will step forward and call me a liar, because we all know this is how things are in the service.

Today as I listen to Glenn Miller's marching music, vintage 1944, it is easy to tell it was not to his liking, because it doesn't sound like him. It just isn't Glenn Miller music that we GIs all loved! Miller, however, had to either play that traditional junk or be sent home in disgrace, which of course would have meant he was finished as a bandleader. After the war, the public would have soured on him, and he knew it.

The killing of Glenn Miller doesn't mean much to the younger generations, but I class it as the biggest loss of World War II. He was the greatest. I still can't believe I was involved in his murder. I was simply doing my job, and so was the Captain.

To prove the 8th Air Force knew what took place, our outfit was put on alert to leave England just eight days after we shot down Glenn Miller's plane. They wanted us out of the picture, so they could further their cover-up without the possibility of any leakage.

We were sitting on the beach in Normandy doing nothing, while London was getting the living hell bombed out of it. So, why was the battery that was best at shooting down V-1 bombs sent to France? Looks – and smells – like a cover up to a killing.

Another reason for sending us to France was that in order for the December 15th story to stick, the 8th Air Force had to remove the guns from the coast. That way, they could remove the danger of Miller being shot down. A significant Allied success unintentionally supported this cover-up angle. Within a couple of months of our arriving in France, the Allies took out the launching sites of the V-1 bombs in Calais.

His plane just took off in fog and was lost en route to France. No guns. No bombs. Just fog. Pure horse hockey!

Chapter 7

Liège and Love

To love and be loved
is to feel the sun from both sides.
David Viscott
1938-1996

Off to Europe

General Timberlake had established his 49th AAA Brigade headquarters in Paris on August 29, 1944 and assumed control of the air defenses of Paris and the Seine River crossings.

On September 17, barely a week after we shot down Glenn Miller's plane, the 134th Battalion received marching orders. In Captain Foley's Morning after Report of September 18th he states:

RECORD OF EVENTS/ALERTED – FOR DEPARTURE.

On September 21st, we left Hythe, Kent by motor convoy, traveling 125 miles to the staging area of our imminent departure. We arrived at Camp Hursley five miles southwest of Winchester, England. There we awaited further departure orders. We received them the next day to depart from Camp Hursley for the port of Southampton.

The convoy departed at 2:15 p.m. By 11:00 that night, we were aboard the Liberty Ship SS JAMES CALDWELL.

We sailed from the docks at Southampton at 8:00 in the morning of September 23rd and anchored off the coast of France at 9:00 p.m. The sea was rough, so we were forced to stay aboard ship until the weather cleared.

On September 25, we began unloading equipment onto barges for landing on Omaha beach. We landed on Omaha Beach September 26, 1944 and suffered no casualties in doing so. Our trucks were waiting for us, and we convoyed to an assembly area and from there we went to our bivouac area and pitched pup tents.

We had a lot of free time, and sports and nightly movies occupied our free time. We didn't even bother to set up our guns because there were no targets or enemy soldiers.

The weather was the big problem, however, as we had no boots and each day the mud got deeper and deeper. It took a contortionist to get into a pup tent, undress and into bed without getting mud on everything or collapsing the tent.

We barely finished building some roads and sidewalks to avoid having to trudge through mud than we received our march orders.

We left Normandy on October 25th and traveled all night and the next day, covering more than 150 miles. En route, we saw only French farm ladies and cows. At one point, a French housewife dumped a full chamber pot out the upstairs window right on top of my head! After that, I was known as "Shithead."

After a night and day on the road, we pitched pup tents in a forest the second night to rest up for our journey to LeMans. The Captain and his lieutenants went into Paris to see the sights. Some of us passed the time selling cigarettes on the black market. To increase our profits, we took dried horse manure, removed the cigarettes from the packets and replaced them with the horse manure. We resealed the packets and sold them to the French.

We all ended up with a fistful of French francs; the only trouble was they gave us counterfeit money. At least, we still had the cigarettes!

Each day, we traveled over a hundred miles, camping near Entampes, France one day, then Laon the next day. At these stops, the men became better acquainted with fine French wine and cognac that nicely took the chill off the night air.

We finally arrived in Namur, Belgium on October 29. We really did very little as there were no planes and we were well behind the front lines.

Liège, Belgium

The city of Liège, nestled below a steep hill, has a long and notable history, dating back to the year 558 and the Roman Empire. Its location has served as a strategic crossroads for armies and uprisings over the centuries. First the Romans ruled, but Liège also fell under the control of the Spanish, French, Dutch and others.

Only after Belgium acquired its independence in the mid-1880s did Liège begin to thrive as a major industrial city, built largely on its steel-making centers. Refortification became a priority, and the redesign featured 12 forts constructed around the city.

Liège lies in the Meuse valley and Ardennes region of Belgium. During World War I, the Germans found this fortressed city a major interference to its plan to move quickly into France. On August 5, 1914, the German invasion reached Liège. The forts succeeded in defending the city briefly but gave up after a lengthy bombardment. Belgian forces eventually surrendered to Germany forces that occupied Liège until the end of the war.

When the Germans returned in 1940, it took only three days to overtake the forts. In 1944, the tide finally turned, and that's where we came in. The United States Army scattered the Germans but the consequence was intense aerial bombing, with more than 1,500 V-1 and V-2 missiles landing in the city between its liberation and the end of World War II.

When we arrived at our new position in Liège, we had a big chateau for headquarters, and the caretaker there kept us supplied with apples and pears. The rest of us pitched our tents. Then it started to rain and rain. Mud was everywhere, which meant that we also had to sleep in the mud. Mud follows the Army.

The gun and range positions were already dug, as we relieved Battery D of the 413th AAA Gun Battalion there. We were now assigned to the 1st Army and the 49th AAA Brigade, under the able command of Brigadier General Timberlake.

On November 1st, we fired on flying bombs that were starting to hit Liège, which was vital to the 1st Army there and the Meuse River crossing, which was the main supply route.

The men found quite a few watering holes in downtown Liège, but I ended up spending my time at Beyne Heusay at a small bar. Here's how that happened. A lot of GIs went there to drink on their time off, but I didn't because I just did not like the taste of alcohol or the effect it had on me.

One night a friend named Rocky, a tall kid who enjoyed drinking, persuaded me to go to the bar. Well, it was better than lying in the mud, so I went. He had told me that the barmaid and her mother owned the bar and that the daughter was really cute. Her name was Citi. He failed to inform me that every GI was making a play for her, but I would soon learn this for myself.

Rocky was talking to her, and now and then she would look my way, causing every bone in my body to turn to jelly. Rocky told me that Citi wanted me to stay and sleep there that night. Somehow I managed to speak. "Oh, yes!" I figured I would be sleeping with her, and I was truly looking forward to it.

I soon learned that all she wanted was my clothes. I stripped, got under the covers and reached for her. No Citi.

Lord, did that featherbed feel good! The next morning, I awoke to find all of my clothes clean and neatly stacked. She had spent the night washing and ironing them for me.

By then, I was convinced I had died and gone to heaven. "Don't send me back down, Lord."

Citi and I never went beyond hugging and kissing. How wonderful that was! I tell you, I was in love.

One night a soldier didn't want to leave the bar at closing time. He wanted a woman. I told him to clear out. I had taken a pistol off a dead German and had it concealed in case the soldier decided to make a move. He did. I had my hand on the pistol and as he lunged for me, I shoved it in his neck and pulled the trigger. Nothing happened. I continued to pull the trigger five more times. I remember his eyes. They seemed to be all white. Suddenly he stopped fighting and ran for the door, never to be seen again. They had no problem with soldiers after that and, strangely, no questions were ever asked.

I took apart the .32 pistol and found that the firing pin was broken. That episode had just about cost me my life. The next night I had my .45, which I wore for the remainder of the war.

Citi and her mother were so grateful to me for protecting them. They couldn't do enough for me. It was embarrassing.

At one point, the gunners were given strict orders not to fire on the V-bombs that were dropping on Liège. It seems that with all the brains the Germans had, they couldn't figure out how to aim their bombs over the target. Their method was to time when the fuel ran out and fill the gas tanks accordingly. They were overshooting Liège and needed some help finding their targets.

Well, our tipsy commanding officer furnished them with all they seemed to need. Of course, we locked on every target with our equipment, but did not fire as ordered.

One night I was on duty and ran through the drill, but when I gave the captain the "fire for effect", he in turn gave the guns the order to fire. Déjà vu all over again.

Four rounds were fired. Down came the V-1 bombs. Oh, we had pulled a bone-headed drunken blunder, because the next day the city of Liège was laid to waste. Thousands were killed. We had given the Germans what they needed. Again, when the powers-that-be read the morning report, they gave us our marching orders, which we expected.

Soon after getting orders one evening, the Captain and a group of his command staff burst into the bar. Up the stairs they came like an FBI raid. This scared the living hell out of Citi and her mother. They had no idea what was taking place. They had only seen the SS troops pull that sort of action.

Citi, fearing the worst and understanding nothing that was going on, ran down to the kitchen and grabbed a 10-inch butcher knife. I saw her run up behind the Captain, draw the knife back and aim it at his back. She was set to kill as many as she could. I lunged at her, grabbed the knife and told her it was all right.

We had just gotten our march order after knocking down the V-1 bombs. My unit just did not want to move out without me. You see the Captain was a good guy and this proved it.

We loaded our equipment and as we were about to pull out, I noticed a cute little girl by the side of the road. She wore a dress and no coat. She was freezing and crying her eyes out. It was Citi. I jumped off the truck and went over to her. That hug and those kisses will never be equaled. It was the most loving, cold, wet embrace a person in love could experience.

She and I had never made love. She said she would, right then and there if that was what I wanted. God, my heart was breaking. By now the convoy drivers were blowing their horns, as we were falling behind. I held Citi close, comforting her as she cried softly in my arms.

When I got back on the truck, not a word was said. Thank God, it was raining. My face was so wet; they couldn't see the tears rolling down my cheeks. My unit knew that it was pure hell for me, and I'm sure many had had the same experience when they left home or somewhere during the war. What a terrible, wonderful experience!

On November 23rd, off to the front lines we went. We were sent as far away as possible from Liège. Why would the Army move us away from where we were so needed? It was like taking fire trucks away from a devastating fire.

Our Captain kept getting drunk, and we kept moving to get away from the problems he caused. Don't get the idea that I didn't like him, because I did. He was a great person, but he couldn't seem to put down the bottle. I really believe I never saw him sober.

Maybe the citizens of Liège would put two and two together and place the blame where it rightfully belonged. Fortunately in time, Liège recovered from the devastation of its steel industry, high unemployment and the attendant problems that both created.

In recent years, Liège has shown some signs of recovery and growth. Aside from social and economic concerns, the life of the city is as colorful as its folk festivals and as boisterous as its nightlife.

I really hated to leave Liège because it was there that I first fell in love, a love that has never been equaled since then. It still brings back the happiest and saddest of memories.

Thank God I knew Citi and learned the meaning of true love. I will never get over her.

Chapter 8

Battle of the Bulge

The master class has always declared
war; the subject class has always
fought the battles. The master class had
all to gain and nothing to lose, while
the subject class had nothing to gain and
everything to lose - especially their lives.
Eugene V. Debs
1855 - 1926

There is no way on earth to describe to someone what the Battle of the Bulge was like. You really had to have been there. The massive scale of the battle was truly staggering to comprehend. Although it lasted only four weeks, it was the most costly battle ever fought, in terms of loss of human lives on both sides.

Mind you, I'm no military historian, but in order to prepare you for the events described in Chapter 9, I felt it was important to put you in the picture of this battle of all battles. Even before the guns fired, the challenges to both sides were immense.

Imagine over a million men (Americans, British and Germans) in a hilly, densely forested area known as the Ardennes region on the Belgian/German border. Now try to imagine fighting the enemy in that situation during the coldest, snowiest winter ever recorded, at least until December 16, 1944, when the Battle of the Bulge started.

Germany had lost significantly on all fronts by the end of 1944, thanks to larger Allied forces and superior technology. That's when Hitler amazed his generals with a bold plan, which he called the Ardennes Offensive, which would give them victory over the weak Allied defenses in that region and allow them to move on to Antwerp and sever the Allies' supply lines.

Although the generals tried to convince Hitler that his plan would not work, he vetoed them and they started to build up their forces for the Offensive, taking troops, even young teenagers, from other front lines. Hitler truly believed that the Americans would die, surrender or flee; putting up a strong defense was furthest from his mind.

The Germans launched their Ardennes Offensive with three powerful armies. They evidently planned well, because American commanders had not envisioned that the Germans would choose such a difficult terrain as the Ardennes for such a battle. The Allied lines were spread thin, concentrating greater forces on the north and south ends of the Ardennes. Divisions, which normally cover five miles, stretched over the 50-mile front.

Needless to say, the German armies – the Wafen SS and Panzer Divisions – completely surprised the American troops, yet they held their ground and fought fiercely. The Malmédy Massacre, in which the Panzer troopers murdered more than 80 American prisoners, put all GIs on notice. The SS killing machine was taking no prisoners. The Americans had only one choice: fight to the death, either theirs or the SS.

Within days the Americans received ample reinforcements that signaled a change of outcome for the Germans. The Red Ball Express ran supplies, such as gas, ammunition and food to the Allies 24 hours a day in a convoy that often came under fire from Nazi troopers manning the roadways.

The goal of the Germans had been to reach the sea, trapping en route several Allied armies and forcing peace negotiations on the Western front. Well, things didn't quite turn out like that. They were unable to reach the Meuse River that snaked along the fringe of the Ardennes.

What the Germans managed to accomplish, however, was the creation of a bulge in the American line that was 70 miles wide and 50 miles deep; hence the Ardennes Offensive has been known ever since as the Battle of the Bulge.

The 106th Infantry Division, which managed to slow down the German advance, played a large part in defeating the German army. By dragging out the battle, the Germans used up valuable equipment and other resources that they were never able to replace. This time lag was vital in the ultimate downfall of the German plans for the Battle of the Bulge. More importantly, it brought an early end to the ravages of World War II in Europe. The 106th Infantry, however, paid dearly for their well-fought part of the Battle, as we will note in the next chapter.

General Eisenhower soon realized that the Offensive was far more than the Americans anticipated. He ordered airborne divisions to the region help the beleaguered troops that were most courageous in checking the SS advance.

Weather eventually grounded the American planes. Instead anyone who could handle a gun was placed on the front lines, as the death toll had brought about a critical shortage of men. The Bulge grew into battle of infantrymen, fighting each other on foot in heavy, hip-deep snow and bitter cold temperatures that often dipped to 45 degrees below zero Slowly, surely, the bulge was closing, destroying most of the German armor in the process.

As it turned out, the Battle of the Bulge, which the Germans started, became the fiercest American battle during World War II, but not without a heavy price. Hitler had miscalculated and instead of realizing victory, he had created a battle scene from hell.

Americans suffered 81,000 casualties, including 23,554 captured and 19,000 killed. More than 100,000 Germans died, were wounded or became prisoners of war. Two hundred British troops were killed. The Germans lost 1,000 aircraft and 800 tanks, and we lost about 800 tanks. That's a lot of equipment that could not be readily replaced on either side in the course of battle.

That's the brief overview of the Battle of the Bulge. Now, we will backtrack a bit to get to the point where I participated – and almost died more than once and was dramatically rescued from behind enemy lines – in this famous World War II battle.

Chapter 9

Behind Enemy Lines

Above all things, never be afraid.
The enemy who forces you to retreat
is himself afraid of you
at that very moment.
André Maurois
1885 - 1967

On November 23, 1944, we left Liège and convoyed to our new position, a bluff overlooking the little village of Losheim, just 800 yards from the enemy line. Two divisions of Hitler's murderous troops that had killed those American prisoners in the Malmédy Massacre, were there, although they were unaware of our arrival.

We encamped on the bluff, which was 500 feet above the village. To our right was a dense, dark pine forest and to our left was the road to Bullingen, located on a flat plain six miles away, where we would go for mail, gas and other supplies.

One had to see the wide-open space where Battery D was dug in. The only landmark was the pine forest. There was nothing a person could orient on except the church steeple below and even that was partly hidden by trees. It was just a vast open landscape spread over acres and acres.

We put up tents and prepared for action, although all was quiet for the first day or two after we arrived. This also happened to be Thanksgiving Day. We had C-ration bars for lunch and turkey dinner that night in the woods in total darkness.

Now a word about darkness, you wouldn't believe how dark darkness can get, unless you've lived in some vast open space with no presence of light except from the moon. We had to learn how to do everything – and go wherever we had to go – in absolute darkness. That, under the threat of coming upon the enemy suddenly, was no picnic.

As soon as we encamped, we also prepared our dugouts. We dug them six feet deep and wired saplings together to make beds. The zigzag entrance covered about 10 feet was designed to save our lives, which ours did. While we were in the hole, we had a little shovel, and we dug our own latrine in the dirt floor.

We really had it made, though: We had five-gallon water cans and a couple of guys had received their Christmas packages early. Urban Eulberg, a Battery D man, who liked to think of himself as an opera singer, received what seemed like a trunk full of fruitcakes from home. He was always passing them out to the other guys.

When the battery had to pull out suddenly after the Bulge started, Captain Foley made Eulberg leave behind his big stash of fruitcakes, much to his dismay. Lives and equipment, in war, are more important that holiday sweets.

Anyway, it sort of embarrassed me when guys offered me some of their goodies, so I never accepted, because I knew I had nothing coming. I couldn't repay them, so why would I eat their treats? I'm strange that way. I guess you could call me a loner.

See I didn't have any buddies or male friends in the service. I really can't explain it. I didn't have any bad experiences with them, but I knew that they did not share the same feelings about certain things. One example was how they talked about the women they had been with, degrading them after receiving the best these pretty young women had to give them. The guys listening just laughed at their stories. I just could never understand this.

I thought they would run me down if I gave them a chance, so I never gave them that chance. Nor did I let them in on my secrets or thoughts about anything.

As far as having a buddy while fighting a war, this has always been my thought: If I'm not smart enough to protect myself, then I don't expect anybody else to protect me. When the going got tough, they would be long gone, so for the most part I worked alone. I had absolutely no fear of being killed. Why? I have no idea.

Back to our story. As we were setting up our equipment, we all looked around and said, "What the hell are we doing here?" We eventually learned that Battery D was to guard the railroad that ran through Losheim to Bullingen and beyond. That happened to be 500 feet down those sheer cliffs. What those old generals had failed to remember was that our 90mm guns would depress only to level, rendering them useless for the purpose of protecting the railroad down such a steep incline.

The battalion commander was relieved of his duties over this mistake. Someone had to pay the price and it surely wasn't going to be some World War I General. I can't complain about the change in command, however, for it just might have saved my life, as you will soon find out.

I was still suffering from saying goodbye to Citi, but I did so not openly so no one would notice. That goes back to my not sharing with the guys. Nevertheless, I was hurting.

Within a couple of days of our arrival, the Germans started shelling our position, but due to their position and ours, they were just missing us by inches. All that firing back and forth we called "mail call."

The first week in December, we claimed several buzz bombs. From then on, the exchange of artillery shells increased to where we were forced to more or less crawl on our bellies down a slope to our mess tent in the forest. The shells were coming over maybe a foot or two from the ground. It was either belly-crawl or get hit by a low flying 88.

The shells were coming in and the night sky was lit up like a 4th of July celebration. You could really read the newspaper by that light.

Bullingen

Several inches of snow were on the ground then and the road leading into our position from Bullingen was muddy as hell. Mud indeed follows the Army.

On my first trip into Bullingen, I noticed that all the people looked fearful. They never extended a gesture of "Glad you're here" or open friendliness toward us GIs. They just went about their business with their heads hung low.

Now I realize Bullingen was only six miles from the Belgian/German border, and deep down these folks probably were suspicious. I'm sure they were wondering which flag to fly – today, the American flag, tomorrow, the German flag. Their lives must have been confusing as hell.

I did notice that the town had suffered little or no damage by the German SS. Normally they would have ripped it apart, so I assumed the SS knew these people to be friendly. Why not? Their friends were German, they spoke German and, last but not least, they were neighbors.

December 7

One day, Rocky, who was with a different battery in the 134th, tempted me. "Let's go AWOL." This meant leaving the encampment without passes. I started walking with him across an open field, then stopped.

"Rocky, this is crazy," I said. "I'm going back."

We were on our way to Liège to see Citi and a girl Rocky had met just before we left.

"What should I tell Citi?" Rocky asked as he kept on walking.

"Tell her I was killed in action."

I knew if I went back, I just might have deserted. That would have meant the firing squad.

Rocky returned a few days later and brought the terrible news that Citi and her mother had been killed by the direct hit of a V-bomb on their bar. This all took place while he was in Liège. This meant, too, that I would have been killed had I gone AWOL with him.

I can't describe how I felt. It was pure awful. Thoughts would come back on the things Citi did for me, like washing my clothes every night and loving me so tenderly.

One night she took me to downtown Liège. We went to a house of prostitution, where she paid the girl and left.

I walked right out behind her and said, "I can't do that." She was happy that I refused.

I had known Citi for less than a month, but it was enough to last a lifetime of sweet memories. You have no idea how many times I have kicked my ass for telling Rocky to tell Citi I was killed in action, but when I turned around to head back to camp, I had no time to come up with any other answer.

I sometimes wonder if it would have been proper for me to be with her when she died. I have never loved another woman like I loved Citi. I have married and divorced twice; it just wasn't fair to those women that I didn't find in them what I had found in my little Liège love, oh, so many years ago.

After a few days, Rocky took off AWOL again, and that was the last I ever saw him. He was either killed by the SS while walking through the fields or picked up as a deserter and shot.

106th Infantry

The 106th Infantry arrived and set up just 150 feet behind our dugouts. By the looks of them, they surely hadn't been off but a few days. I guess they couldn't believe what they saw, because it was so quiet. No rifle fire, but maybe just five or six rounds of 88 shells aimed at our location. We really got to the point where we paid little attention to them.

Instead of digging foxholes, they brought out the baseballs, bats and gloves and started playing catch, laughing and having a good time.

It seems that the Germans did not know the 106th had moved in, as all the shelling was coming in on us. Suddenly, the shelling increased and became more accurate. All the time our guns sat silent with their protective covers over them.

A thought crossed my mind. Could there be a spotter in that church steeple across the deep canyon below? We were on high ground, and I could more or less look down on the steeple. This meant that if there was a spotter, he could not see us as we were over a slight rise in the ground.

Being an independent bastard, I removed the cover from my M-51 and proceeded to lay some 50-caliber rounds into that steeple. I started low and went up so I could cut off the spotter's escape.

Oh, Lord, here comes Captain Foley, face all flushed. "What the hell are you doing?" he demanded.

I explained the purpose of the shelling, and he just nodded and returned to the Command Post (CP).

As I was firing, the artillery shelling slowed then halted. That meant there had indeed been a spotter in the steeple. The 88s weren't accurate to begin with. All the shells hit over into the valley behind our position.

Once an 88 shell hit the latrine, covering a guy I had no use for with all of its contents. He was a mess! Talk about being pissed off when I poked fun at him. He just had no sense of humor. He could have gotten into real trouble from infection, because there just was no running up and down the roads looking for a field hospital for him. To this day, I laugh about that episode.

He may have had reason for his bitterness, because he had relatives just across the deep canyon where I gunned down the church steeple. Can you believe the luck of pulling into a new location only to realize, hey, I have family over here?

I'm really surprised he didn't shoot me, the hatred was that intense. I was the only one who stood up to him.

Enemy tracks

As it was, a young GI and I walked behind enemy lines about three miles. There we came upon Tiger tank tracks and hob-nailed boot tracks. We could sense we were right in the center of a German tank outfit, so we did an about face and got out of there.

The only thing that saved our lives was that the Germans were massing for an attack – the Battle of the Bulge. Their tanks were dug in and brush covered them so well that we could not see them. The SS could have killed my partner and me, but didn't or they would have revealed their position and plan.

When I saw those tracks, I said, "Don't act alarmed. Just turn around and return to the outfit." I'm sure we would have been taken prisoner or had our throats cut to keep us quiet. It was a narrow escape, indeed!

We reported back to the CP, and the Captain must have reported the news to the battalion headquarters, because the unit moved out the next night. Just maybe our findings saved all of Battery D, because the SS was under orders to take no prisoners and to kill every American they came upon.

I walked back and told the 106th and told them that it would be best for them to clean up their rifles and dig in. I explained the tracks the other fellow and I had found behind enemy lines.

The 106th laughed at me and continued to play ball. After all, it was very quiet on the front, except for us firing a few shells into the German lines and getting occasional return fire from them.

Sudden surprises

Only a few times was I really scared and one occurred a few days before the SS attacked our position. A German ME262 came over us at treetop level. It was late afternoon, and the fog and bad weather had not moved in yet. I'm sure someone was in that jet taking photographs of our position.

The sound of this jet was something none of us had ever heard before. It scared the living hell out of us, because we well remembered what the buzz bomb did to a city block in London. Surely a jet bomber could do worse damage.

That night, I was on guard duty and my post was in the dark forest. And I mean dark. All of a sudden, a plane flew overhead. Suddenly, I heard something crashing through the pine trees right above me and down slid a German paratrooper so close to me that he brushed me as he landed.

I held him at gunpoint. I surprised him, but when he spoke in broken English, he surprised me, too. He said he was a British paratrooper, but I knew he was a spy. I conducted a search and found a radio transmitter plus other spy equipment but no weapon on him. Now, mind you, I could not see my hand in front of my face, as there was absolutely no available light.

All at once, I heard the paratrooper cry and beg me to let him escape, as he had two young daughters. I was very tempted to release him. Hell, no one would have ever known, but I did my duty, found the command post and turned him over. I knew all spies were taken out and shot. No trial, no hearings, just shot!

To this day, I'm sorry I marched him to the CP. I should have stripped him, given him a kick in the ass and set him free. He cried that he wasn't a real spy but was sent on the mission because he spoke English. That has bothered me all these years. I held his life in my hands, and he had to leave those two little girls. War isn't fun and games.

What seemed strange to me was that when I captured the spy, not a single man in our outfit said, "Nice going" or even questioned me about it. They were all quiet. Later I realized that they were scared.

Shortly after that all hell broke loose. The air was full of bursting shells. The Germans were putting a move on our position.

Enemy alert!

At about 10 a.m. on the morning of December 16th we received word to be on alert for enemy patrols in the area. The guard was increased. In the afternoon, the artillery fire quieted down and we likened the lull to the calm before a storm.

We were right. That night the German breakthrough began, the spearhead striking in our immediate area. First the battery was alerted and all secret fuses were removed. Battery

D received orders to move the range equipment out and finally the entire battery was given marching orders at 11 p.m. that night, forced by enemy action to withdraw.

John Pfeister
Battery D

Unbeknownst to the four of us, Battery D moved out, leaving a ¾-ton truck for us to use in our escape. Much later I learned that as the radar was pulled out of its position, an 88 shell scored a direct hit on the radar emplacement right after the radar was moved.

John Pfeister was there and almost got killed. Fortunately, no one was hurt, and after a brief delay in moving the equipment out of the muddy lane, the battery continued its strategic retreat under the nose of Hitler's famous Panzer Division and other crack Wermacht troops.

The four of us in the dugout were within five feet of the radar, and there were so many shells coming in, we didn't even know it. One question keeps nagging at me. How did radar pull out and leave us in the dugout? They drove right past us and never bothered to tell us they were leaving.

Massacre

The Germans were close and coming toward us. This was the start of the Bulge, and being that we were closer to the German line than the other troops, our position got hit first. Of course, there were just the four of us left, but the SS didn't know that yet.

Tracer bullets filled the air, so the four of us ducked into our dugout. We could hear tanks and trucks, and then we heard the screams, as the GIs begged for their lives, the boys of the 106th. The SS shot them in cold blood. We knew they were all were dead when the shooting stopped.

I'm sure very few people have heard the screams and pleadings of the dying. It is an awful sound. You never forget it, and you surely never want to hear it again.

These poor boys had just arrived from the States and didn't have their rifles ready for battle. I had told them they were on the front line with no protection in front of them and urged them to put away the balls and bats, because the tracks I found meant the enemy was very close. Of course, this meant very little to them, because it was so hushed on the front, simply because the Germans were preparing to attack.

Later on, as fate would have it, the dead bodies of the 106th Infantry would save my life!

SS attack!

One of the standing orders from Army headquarters if the enemy approached was to destroy our highly secret cable that carried data from the radar to the M-10 director. That became my responsibility. I slipped out of our dugout revetment and with a knife proceeded to cut up the cable.

Suddenly there was a flash and a bang! An SS trooper shot me point blank and hit me in the upper lip. We were trained to keep our .45 sidearm cocked at all times, so out of pure instinct, I fired as an SS troop was reloading.

I returned to the dugout bleeding like a stuck hog, as we used to say on the farm. I wrapped something around my mouth to stop the bleeding.

I was bleeding badly and called for an aid man, but the phone was dead. It stands to reason that leaving four soldiers under such precarious conditions bode ill for us.

The exchange of shots and my return, bleeding, told the other guys that shit was about to hit the fan. They seemed frozen, not offering to assist or even offering a word. They were all pale as ghosts. I especially remember George Allan Dripps. The expression on his face was something else!

Of course, I couldn't talk because I was holding onto my upper lip, hoping to stop the flow of blood. None of us could really talk, as the SS would hear us. I'm sure they knew someone was in the dugout.

To this day, I don't understand why I crawled out of that dugout to follow orders and sabotage our highly secret cable. At least in the process, I took out one of those cold-blooded murderers. We knew the SS was still in the area, and they knew someone was in our dugout.

Tank attack!

Now we hear what turned out to be a Tiger tank pull up outside our dugout. All was quiet. Suddenly the tank engine revved up and KABOOM! The roof of our homemade dugout raised and fell right back in place. The SS had shot an 88 into our dugout crawlway.

We owe our lives to some forgotten sergeant that had told us to crisscross the crawlway. The tank driver could not lower his gun, so the shell hit nothing but solid dirt, yellow Belgian clay!

After the tank attack, the SS picked up the dead body of the trooper that attacked me, and then they backed up their tank onto our truck and fired an 88 round into our revetment, trapping us in our underground trench. That really saved our lives. Had they fired a high-explosive round, we would have all been killed, so we were thankful for that dumb gunner!

Of course, this was one hell of an explosion, but it did not have the effect the German jet had in terms of fear. Our only light came through an opening in the tree limbs we used to construct our roof.

By now, it was snowing and I was still bleeding, so I dug a small hole and scraped in fresh snow and pressed it to my lip. That must have saved me from bleeding to death, because the shot had nicked an artery. To this day, I sometimes get numbness in my lip.

As soon as the tank left, we started digging with our hands very quietly, of course. By the sound of it, all our GIs were either dead or had escaped, so we sat wondering what to do next. Of course, we didn't know at the time that we were stranded. We later learned the SS was killing everyone, taking no prisoners.

The short straw

Approximately three days after the tank attack on our dugout, suddenly we heard someone outside, moving down our crawlway. We were about to open fire when Sgt. George Delaney yells out, "Don't shoot!"

We were relieved someone had come back for us, but we soon had our hopes dashed. Delaney had left the battery days earlier to find an aid station; he was either sick or injured. He had gone to Bullingen, when the Wafen SS hit there. He was stranded there and hid out in a cellar for a couple of days.

Delaney then managed to infiltrate the German lines and joined the 1st Infantry Division, and from there he made is way back to our position. When he arrived, he found no one, just the truck that the tank had used to shoot our dugout.

That night, he crawled out and off he went in pitch-black darkness. He later told of us about his experience. When morning came, he spotted a house and went to the basement, only to stumble over a live body. The basement was full of GIs, all with their hand grenade pins pulled out. If the German SS came, their plan was to blow up the house, as they too had heard the SS was taking no prisoners.

As morning came, they heard tanks, which stopped at the house and unloaded. An SS trooper came down the stairs with a flashlight that had very weak batteries. When he saw nothing, he turned around and went back up the stairs. All the GIs had pulled their grenade pins and had to replace them in the dark. The SS soon pulled out, and that night Delaney was back on the railroad tracks.

This experience was truly amazing for the simple reason he had no idea where our outfit was. He soon learned that he had walked over 50 miles; that's how far behind the lines we were. Somehow he made it, traveling only at night, of course.

Delaney was exhausted from lack of sleep and was scared to death, because that night he did not sleep a wink. He just seemed to rock back and forth the whole time. He was in shock.

Sleep was not a high priority for any of us then anyway. We had a choice of sleeping on dirt or on telephone wires. That might sound uncomfortable, but at least the wires kept you off the damp ground.

The next day, we set out to plan our own escape. Delaney, who was assigned to the Supply detail and was the ranking member among us, said one of us would have to steal out when it became dark and go for help.

His duties made him more familiar with a wider range of the area than we were. He knew where the railroad tracks were and drew a map. The railroad tracks were located at the bottom of those sheer cliffs, so steep that I was afraid to look over the edge.

We drew straws (not really straws, but sticks from our roof), and wouldn't you know it, Delaney pulled the short straw! I can tell you one thing. If I had drawn the short straw, all of us would have died, because I had lost too much blood. No way could I have been able to walk any distance in search of our outfit.

After dark, without a word, Delaney left the dugout. How he climbed down the cliff and was not killed, I'll never know. Mind you, he had no pickaxe like folks today use in ordinary mountain climbing. He had no light, either. He had to move only in darkness, as the SS was all around us. One slip up and he'd either get shot or fall at least 500 feet or more!

We were left behind to wait, realizing but not speaking our thoughts that the chances of Delaney getting through the SS lines alive was next to none. Even if he managed to get back, who would dare to come out to rescue us? We were safe for the time being, as we had sufficient rations and water, but how long would we wait?

A miraculous rescue

When Delaney reached the outfit and told headquarters there were still men alive behind enemy lines, it just so happened – as I now believe – a Colonel with G2 (Army Intelligence) happened by and learned of our predicament. Fluent in German and armed with the fake official paperwork he would need to get through SS checkpoints, he left on a truly daring rescue mission.

The only guidepost about our location was a field of dead GI bodies from the 106th Infantry. Delaney told him our dugout was nearby. The site was at the edge of a forest with no main roads in the area, only a dirt road that led back to our location.

Colonel Israel, who attempted this daring rescue, had guts plus brains. He knew we were facing certain death if we attempted to walk out ourselves. He mounted a 2½-ton U. S. Army truck and struck out alone. Bear in mind he had perhaps 50 miles littered with SS checkpoints to pass – both ways!

From three to five days after Delaney left to find help, we heard the sound of a truck engine. We removed the safety from our rifles and pointed them at the crawl space.

All of a sudden, all we could see in the dim light were two shiny oak leaf emblems, as a man crawled into our space, ordering, "Don't shoot! I'm Colonel Israel. I'm your new commanding officer!" Then, looking at my bloodstained shirt, he said, "My God!" He must have thought I had received a chest wound, not just a nick in the lip.

Colonel Israel ordered us out of the trench and onto the truck. He told us to lie face down on the truck bed. "There are a lot of frozen dead bodies of GIs out there," he explained. "I'm going to cover you with those bodies. At one of the SS checkpoints, you might get poked with a bayonet when the guards try to make sure all the bodies are dead. If you get poked, bite your lip and don't move. If you don't, we are all dead." He spoke in a calm, self-assured manner.

We climbed into the truck and did as we were told. He then proceeded to cover us with the frozen bodies of the dead GIs. Thank God it was below zero so no body fluids dripped or oozed out of them.

When we were all loaded up, the Colonel drove off, knowing just how to return to our outfit. I remember thinking, how can he get by the Wafen SS with dead Americans in the truck? He had a plan, and it worked.

I have no idea how far we drove or how many roadblocks we were stopped at, but it seemed endless. Colonel Israel chewed those SS soldiers out for whatever reason I don't know. It put the troopers on the defensive, and rather than face punishment for disobeying orders, they let him pass. At times under my breath, I wished he would go easier on the SS, for fear they might shoot him out of anger.

As he had explained to us in the dugout, though, to get through the roadblocks, he was planning to tell the SS that he was going into the American lines, gathering up members of his command. The SS bought it, partly because of his fluency of German and partly because of the way he barked at them. The Germans were using our trucks and uniforms, pretending to be Americans, so he just reversed the trick.

I have to give Colonel Israel a lot of credit. He was fearless in his conversations with the SS, barking back at them. The SS were pure killers, so it was best not to let on that you were afraid in any way. Plus they knew this was their last stand. That is why after the war, I removed some front teeth whenever they refused to obey my orders.

In due time we arrived back safely at our outfit. The Colonel worked alone, pulling the dead bodies off of us. No one came to his aid.

When we got off the truck, he shook our grimy hands, and we saluted him. We didn't expect anyone to greet us, and we weren't disappointed. No one – including Captain Foley – came to welcome us back.

When we got back to our unit, everybody just went back to their normal duties and positions, so we seldom saw each other. During combat, it's not a picnic. You were on duty 24 hours a day or you would end up dead, so there was little gathering about over coffee to discuss details.

We received no explanation why the battery pulled out without telling us they were leaving, so we could hop on the truck. During the writing of this book, I did come across a story that four or five GIs were left behind at all the batteries to pick up the last of the equipment. I have no idea if this is true or what happened to the others left behind.

[Captain Foley received a Bronze Star for making it through the war without having any of his Battery D troopers killed in action. I should have received a Purple Heart for being wounded in the line of duty, damaging that secret cable at the order of Army headquarters. But, when I saw that men lost legs and arms in the war, I just didn't have the heart to try to get a medal for being shot in the lip!]

Delaney was back in charge of Supply and his truck was nearby the CP. I walked over and thanked him. "How the hell did you make it back?" I asked.

I never did get his story. He just smiled and issued me clean clothes. I stripped down, standing right there in the snow. Of course, my socks and shoes were soaked, but I was used to that. He didn't have any blankets, but at least it was good getting out of those blood-soaked clothes and into some clean, dry ones.

Delaney was one of the best guys a person would want to know. He was very quiet and extremely brave, although he never acted the part. [I was saddened that, although George Delaney is still alive, he has almost no memory of events of the war. I had hoped when I found him that he would be able to tell me how he made his way back to our outfit.]

I don't remember even having a cup of coffee that day. The mess sergeant hated my ass, because the day before the SS hit, I was singing, "The Germans are coming! The Germans are coming!"

Well, he was a yellow bastard and was scared to death. He drew back a huge serving spoon to whack me on the back of my head.

I said, "Go ahead, you son-of-a-bitch. I have been wanting to whip your ass."

He didn't complete his swing, which saved him from an ass kicking. Of course, this meant there was no need for me to go to the mess tent because he controlled the food.

We were very lucky to have lived through the Bulge. Back with our outfit, we were sitting in an open field and the weather was zero or near that. I was so tired after losing so much blood; I just had to get some sleep. The problem was I had no blanket, so I had to locate a place where tanks wouldn't run over me.

I located a small creek. It didn't give me complete protection, but it was better than nothing. Oh, boy, when I woke up, I couldn't feel anything. Then I discovered my hip was frozen in the ice. I tried to break the ice with my rifle butt, but the ice was solid. There I was frozen in the creek! I assume anybody that might have come upon me would take me for another dead body to be picked up later by the detail that collected the dead.

I worked and tugged and tried to get the circulation going in my legs. It was so cold the ice wouldn't give. I knew I couldn't expect help from anyone, so I finally broke loose, leaving a lot of skin frozen to my fatigue pants. I didn't see an aid man. What could he have done?

I didn't get my lip sewn up until a year later, when John Finegan put two stitches in it with a needle so dull he could barely pull through my lip with no novocaine to deaden the pain. Until then, my lip would bleed whenever I laughed, but I learned to keep it under control.

All right, let's jump ahead a bit so we can finish with stories about my shot-up lip. Months later, our battery clerk requested the traveling dentist to come out to the field to examine my teeth, because I complained that my lip would not heal. Unfortunately, this trip cost the hefty dentist and his driver their lives.

After he finished with me, I warned him not to take a certain road out, because there was a gunner that way and he would sure as hell send an 88 shell as soon as they hit the road.

The dentist insisted on going that way anyway, and within a few minutes, he and his driver were dead. Until that time, I had never seen an overweight man go straight up in the air 15 feet. Of course, there went all my dental records, too.

Christmas Eve, 1944

I don't recall the exact date that Colonel Israel rescued us, but we were back with Battery D by Christmas Eve. Like good soldiers, we went right to work, manning our guns. Enemy aircraft attacked, strafing convoys and trying to bomb strategic crossroads. Our M-51 Quadmounts engaged the planes and managed to down one of them.

In the midst of the loud booms and bangs of war, we heard a mother and her three little ones softly singing Christmas carols in a barn behind us. It sounded so beautiful!

Suddenly six Tiger tanks rumbled up the road towards our dug-in Quads and fired at us. Instead, they hit only the barn behind us, killing the mother and her children. The shell hit them directly and the singing stopped. That turned out to be one very sad night. Why do people have to kill each other?

What saved us was that someone called back to the 2nd Armored Division and a self-propelled cannon came sliding up and opened fire. Lucky for all of us, the tanks turned tail and fled.

I firmly believe the Germans, including the SS, were simply tired of killing or they would have never turned tail.

Christmas 1944

Holidays in wartime are most unpredictable. Ours was observed in a rather unusual setting, but we still had turkey with all the trimmings, and a big mail call. American light, medium and heavy bombers and fighter planes of all types filled the air all day, leaving long white vapor trails in the cold December sky.

On December 26th, we moved to a new position just west of Verviers, Belgium. The range section joined us and we had an AA mission again. We stayed here for three days then moved to Eupen, Belgium on the 29th. We were attached to the 413th AAA Gun Battalion in a field that night until they moved out. The next day we assumed position and began building shacks and getting German huts to live in.

We spent quite a bit of time in Eupen. While we were there, we got day passes to Verviers and 48-hour passes to Eupen, according to the battalion clerk's reports.

There were still no pretty Hollywood girls to entertain us, but we did see one pianist. She was so scared; she had to give it up because there was so much dirt and other crap covering most of her body from the shelling. Only a few of us were there, but we gave her a big hand. At least, she tried.

Ruhr Area, Germany

Our M-51 guns fired on enemy aircraft and downed one. Other than that, January 1944 was a fairly quiet month, but it would not last long. We were in the Ruhr Area, Germany's industrial heartland.

Then artillery fire picked up significantly. In fact, for a time, the shelling was worse than we encountered in the Battle of the Bulge. Of course, we were all dug into our foxholes.

When people say the ground shook, well, the roar of artillery fire actually did move my body against the sides of my foxhole. I didn't poke my head above ground until the firing eased up the next morning.

My Lord! When I raised up, right there within an inch of me was a dead horse. It had had its guts blown out. All that remained were his two rear legs, part of his chest, neck and head. Its eyes were so full of fear and pain; the sight really gave me a start.

I'm glad it was winter, because there were dead soldiers, civilians and farm animals with their pain-filled eyes staring up at us. Most of them were gunshot, a horrible death.

Another story that stands out in my mind was the one involving paratroopers. It seems that some commanding officer of a paratrooper group that had never actually jumped in Europe decided to do a practice jump. Supposedly the CO didn't inform the CO on the ground of his plan.

Suddenly I saw hundreds of paratroopers being dropped on the American line. I assumed they were Germans and opened fire with my M-51. I was the only one shooting at them, as far as I know. In fact, I was confused as to why no one else was concerned about paratroopers being dropped in our midst.

No one came and asked what I was shooting at. I finally got tired of shooting paratroopers. No one ever said anything to me about the incident.

Chapter 10

Ludendorff Bridge/Remagen

If you are in any contest,
you should work as if there were –
to the very last minute –
a chance to lose it.
Dwight D. Eisenhower
1890 - 1969

It is now March 1945, and the war is nearing its end. At least, that was our hope. Our 90mm Gun Battalion just happened to be a short distance from Remagen, where the Ludendorff Bridge is located. Our commanding officer gave us our marching orders, and you could tell by the sound of his voice that we were headed for an important mission.

Of course, no lighting was allowed, but we had been well trained to work in the darkness. The only light we had was from all the tracers and artillery shells exploding. Within a short time, we could hear a battle taking place a few miles ahead.

It seems that a very brave sergeant, Alex A. Drabik, crossed the Ludendorff Bridge that already had been set with charges to blow it up. Knowing that he was able to cross it was great news. It meant that we had a bridge across the Rhine!

Now, again to put you in the picture, you'll need to know a little background on the Ludendorff Bridge and its importance to the Allies at that point in time. The 1,069-foot Ludendorff Bridge was built across the Rhine River during World War I, connecting Remagen and Erpel, Germany.

Ludendorff was one of the finest steel railroad spans and also an important strategic site in World War II. Miraculously, it was the last bridge standing over the Rhine by the time we arrived on the scene. It's no wonder that General Eisenhower said Ludendorff Bridge was "worth its weight in gold."

Not that the Germans hadn't tried to demolish it. The Third Reich was facing defeat in 1945 when Hitler ordered his fighters to stall the Allied advance by destroying all bridges across the Rhine. They succeeded in destroying 22 road bridges and 25 railroad bridges, but several attempts to collapse the Ludendorff Bridge failed.

On March 7, 1945, the 9th US Armored Division, commanded by Lt. Karl Timmermann, reached Ludendorff. The taking of this bridge has become known in war annals as the "Miracle of Remagen."

My outfit was a few miles from the river when a Jeep slid up and two MPs jumped out, yelling, "We need a machine gun. The 9th Infantry just took the bridge!"

My M-51 was hooked onto a half-track, and we went full speed after the Jeep in pitch darkness. By tracer light my ammo man, Salvatore Rancatore, and I saw the bridge. Someone there directed us to park at the entrance to the bridge and pick up muzzle blasts and machine gun tracers across the Rhine.

Bursting artillery shells and tracer bullets gave us plenty of light to set up. We started firing before the half-track driver unhooked us.

Only the 9th Infantry and a couple of their Jeeps were at the bridge with us. Stories abound that say there were AAA guns all over the place. These are bar stories that you hear at the American Legion or VFW after downing a beer and a shot of bourbon. This is why I don't belong to any clubs. Too many heroes.

Sure, after the bridge was secured and the traffic thinned out, some guns must have moved behind us, but I didn't see them. In the beginning, though, only the assigned divisions were allowed in the convoy.

Rancatore was new at ammo detail and was scared to death. He did a great job, considering the circumstances, but being new he could have gotten us killed, and he almost did.

I told Rancatore to keep low, but he didn't and caught one in the head. Soon after, just as dawn was breaking, I caught a glimpse of something out of the corner of my eye. I swung my .45 around and saw a man on the ground. I was about to fire, when he yelled, "I'm American!"

I was a little edgy because Rancatore had just caught one in the head and I was trying to wipe his blood off my face.

I'm second from the left, with my fellow Battery D gunners
(L to R) Pfc. William F. Miller, Pfc. Harold H. Doty
and my ammo man, Pfc. Salvatore Rancatore.

"Who are you?" I yelled but not in such proper language. To Rancatore, I shouted, "Why didn't you tell me he was behind me?" Both of them were very shook up, because that is how people don't survive a war.

There was no way to hear their replies over the noise of my gun, but by then I could see that the man on the ground was sketching all the action going on around us. He explained later that he was H. Charles McBarron, an illustrator with the 1st Army. He apologized for slipping up behind us.

"You're both very lucky to be alive, because I won't put up with that. It's my life I'm concerned about."

Things let up a bit and he showed me some of his work. I got busy doing my job, and when I checked on him again, he was gone. I had really gotten off on him for slipping up behind us, because if I had not noticed what he was doing, I would have had no choice but to shoot him. To stay alive in war, you don't trust anyone, even if he appears to be friendly.

In hindsight, he was one brave soul for lying on the ground, unafraid of getting hit by all the bullets zinging around our position.

[Years later, I tried to locate him, but I had no luck. Then one day, I opened *WW2*, a semi-monthly magazine to which I subscribe. I was completely stunned to find the exact scene he had drawn complete with me manning the Quadmount at the entrance to the Ludendorff Bridge! I was sad to learn that McBarron, who had captured our soldiers in war, died before I could catch up with him again.]

Rancatore went back to our unit to get patched up, leaving me alone. I had to load the shells myself until I got a replacement. Our machine gun was still the only one at the bridge. It scares me now, but back then I was not scared one little bit. I had no problem staying awake, as there were plenty of fireworks to keep me awake.

The M-51 cockpit was very comfortable and catching a catnap posed no problem. I shot a lot of shells in between naps. The M-51 was self-contained; we had storage for C-rations and plenty of water and ammo, so I was all right. It was quite an experience.

The self-propelled tank destroyer on the bridge broke through shortly after we took the bridge. The 9th Infantry was the only one crossing the bridge, but soon seven divisions caught up with the rest of them.

You had to be proud of those boys, because they were running full speed to get across the bridge, knowing damned well if they were cut off it would spell certain death for them. Now, they were the real heroes of the day!

Immediately afterward, the Germans made several attempts to destroy the bridge by bombing and using frogmen. In fact, according to historical accounts, Nazi frogmen kept trying to sabotage the bridge.

You had no idea how many tanks, trucks, guns and personnel passed in front of me. When that tank destroyer broke through the planking, everything stopped. All the traffic had to get the hell out of there, because they were all bunched up and would have been one hell of a target for artillery and planes.

I just wonder how far the traffic was backed up; my guess is over 50 or 60 miles, at least. A normal person cannot fathom the power of the United States.

I forget how many days it took for almost 105,000 men to cross, but it seemed like I never got relief. The only trucks allowed back over the bridge were the dead wagons and ambulances. This included generals.

When word came that the bridge was secure, General Bull, one of those crusty old generals left over from World War I, said, "So what?" He surely would have preferred seeing a lot of Germans on that bridge when it collapsed, because he had that body-counting way of looking at war.

As George Rogers, one author of these times that I ran across in my research, wrote, "If the Germans had counterattacked between 4:00 and 5:00, the bridgehead would have been wiped out." How true!

ME262 - the German fighting jet

Two days after we took the bridge, two US Army P38s planned to bring down one of those ME262 German fighter jets as it attempted to bomb the bridge. If you remember, one of those fighter jets almost shook us out of our boots during the Battle of the Bulge.

The Luftwaffe made them available too late in the war. The jet engine could not sustain but a few hours of use before becoming inoperable. Since the Germans had a difficult time getting parts and petrol, most of the Luftwaffe and the 262s were eventually grounded.

I believe John Pfeister, the younger, said it best. Had the Germans developed the ME262 and the V-2 [replacing the V-1 buzz bomb] at the beginning of the war, the outcome would have been different, for sure. The Germans would have been writing the history books instead of us.

Back to the incident at the Ludendorff Bridge. The P38s knew they could not match the flying speed of the ME262, so their plan was to climb high over the Rhine and when a ME262 made its bombing run, dive on it at full speed. Well, it did not work out as planned.

The pilots made their dives, one from the East overhead and the other coming from the West. The problem was that the ME262 was long gone as the pilots went over the Rhine. As a result, the American pilots were forced to pull out of their dives. They both did the same maneuver. They hit head on and crashed into the freezing Rhine, killing both pilots.

I knew the Americans were not equipped to match the power and speed of the ME262. I had a very hard time trying to keep up with it firing tracer bullets, even if I shot them out in front of the jet.

The main thing – we took the bridge and saved thousands of lives because without that, the crossing would have to have been made via boats. Due to the advantage of the mountain on the German side, our men would have been slaughtered.

That's why General Eisenhower was so happy we took it. The remaining bridge tower on the shore near where I placed my M-51 Quadmount is now a peace museum.

Rhine – or wine – crossing

In the area of the Ludendorff Bridge there were wineries on both sides of the river. On my side there was just wine; champagne was on the other side.

We had an old soldier, George Wargo, who had 28 years of service in the Army, and he drank away 27 and a half of them. It seems the wine on our side just wasn't strong enough; he needed something with more kick. He thought just maybe that champagne across the Rhine would do the trick.

Somewhere he and another drunken buddy found a wheelbarrow and struck out across the river to get a load of booze. Now this meant holding up all the tanks, trucks, Jeeps and other traffic.

I didn't see the trip across, but I did see the return trip, and it is just a shame it wasn't recorded on film. They had champagne stacked in that wheelbarrow and, of course, again all the traffic was held up and the GIs were laughing and yelling, officers included. It was hilarious.

I used a newly dug (and unused) latrine to store the champagne that surely deteriorated unless someone was lucky enough to have found it. When I hid the bottles I had the presence of mind to tip them downward so the corks would stay wet. To discourage anyone from digging them up, I mixed toilet paper with the dirt when I covered up the bottles. What a waste of great champagne, but I couldn't take it with us.

Collapse of the Ludendorff Bridge

On March 17, 1945, 10 days after we captured the Ludendorff, it suddenly collapsed, but not before seven US divisions crossed over it. There lay the bridge in the Rhine.

My gun moved to the other side within a few feet of the bridge when it collapsed. There was an awful silence, then Rancatore looked at me and said, "I'll be damned." That shows how quickly war can harden a person.

The collapse killed more than 28 Army engineers that were trying to strengthen the bridge. They all went down with the bridge. Many were cut in half by the collapsing ironwork. There was absolutely nothing any of us could do. Probably most of them died without uttering a sound; it happened so fast.

People throughout history since then have claimed that they jumped into the Rhine to try to save the engineers. Horse hockey; they would have died almost instantly in the process due to the swift and cold currents.

I have great respect for these engineers. They had a terrible duty, but they did it well. Fortunately before their deaths, they had reinforced our position by building pontoon bridges to make crossings easier.

The capture of the Ludendorff Bridge enabled Americans to pour men and equipment onto the other side of the Rhine for 10 crucial days.

The American success at Ludendorff did not set well with Hitler. Indeed, he managed to have four of his officers court-martialed and executed. The fifth officer would have met the same fate had he not already become one of our POWs.

For their part in capturing the bridge, all the men in the 27th Armored Infantry Battalion received a medal, which they absolutely deserved. Being part of a bastard outfit like mine, however, Rancatore and I didn't get even a pat on the back. There had been only one machine gun at the bridge, and that was the one that the two of us manned.

Back to Remagen

Soon we moved back to Remagen, just a few miles from our position. Now the war was winding down, because the Germans were retreating so fast you could only pick up the wounded and the ones that simply stopped fighting.

We were sitting right in the center of what seemed to be the wine capital of wineries. If you weren't drunk, you had a problem swallowing or hated wine. In fact, if the Germans only knew what was going on there, they could have returned and won the war, as we were all drunk every day as soon as our duties died down.

That's when I developed a taste for wine, and it helped a lot. I was still thinking about Citi every minute.

A fellow named Roush finally joined me as a replacement for Rancatore. Now Roush was drunk all the time. Once, he crawled into a mattress cover and fell fast asleep. As it turned out, this took place in a field when a V-2 hit a few yards away right in the middle of a flock of sheep. There went sheep and dogs flying 50 feet into the air! I was untouched, but the dirt from the explosion nearly buried Roush.

Soon a dead wagon came skidding up, and I just then got a target, but they were asking about him.

"Is he dead?" they yelled.

"Yeah, dead drunk," I yelled back.

All they heard was "dead", as the noise of my gun covered the rest of my response. I looked down, and they assumed he was dead and took him away. I never saw him again.

To this day, when someone says, "Roush", I jump. I really believe he was buried alive.

It was great when I was finally relieved and got some sleep. The house I lived in was the home of the local miller, and it was truly a mansion. He had a daughter about 19. Well, you-know-who latched onto her but only after I kicked another GI in the chest, sending him down the stairs. You know he never liked me after that, but I could not have cared less.

One night, this little story developed. One of the boys in Battery D never had luck getting a girl, so in one of the houses we took over we found a lot of women's clothing. One of our guys dressed up as a woman.

It was dark outside, and he found the unlucky fellow in a truck and slid in beside him. You had to be a first class nut not to know this guy was not a woman because of his beard.

The prank didn't work because to the surprise of all of us secretly watching this show, the guy tore into this dressed-up "girl" and there was a quite a tussle to break his hold. It finally dawned on us that the guy was homosexual, who thought the "girl" was one, too!

We laughed so hard we cried. We honestly had not known his sexual orientation prior to putting the prank together. Anyway, it had been a long time between laughs, so we really enjoyed ourselves that night.

Another night when all was quiet, we got word that we were going to rob the local bank. I was surprised to see all the officers, including the captain. Well, we aimed our 90mm guns at the vault, and the desired effect resulted. The door was gone and there went the looters, like hogs running for corn.

I don't know why, but I did not participate, probably because there wasn't anything to buy. All the stores had been looted by the displaced persons settling up old debts, so what would I do with any money?

Well, one of the older and wiser guys had a plan in mind, because he took bails of money and after the war he went to Garmisch Partenkirichen and purchased a resort hotel.

Hell, we young guys never had any money so we didn't have incentives like that. That was where age came in handy, because he was the oldest man in our outfit. Captain Foley, who was quite a character, was laughing because he had built a fire using the 30,000 marks he had grabbed in the heist.

I was running low on wine one night and decided to get a load. It was pitch-black, but I knew my way around.

As I approached the wine cellar, I heard some drunken GI yell out, "This is my cellar!" Then a rifle butt smashed against the door, just inches from my head. I had only my sidearm but rather than shoot, I kicked him in the gut and he fell 17 feet to the bottom into at least four feet of wine.

In their haste to get wine in the dark, the GIs simply used their submachine guns to shoot holes in these huge kegs. They would then hold their canteen cups to catch the stream of wine. As a result all those holes, the wine leaked faster than it could go down the drain or into their cups.

After the GI hit bottom, I never heard a sound, so I assumed he became a casualty. I just went to another cellar. There was nothing I could do, because he had already let me know he wanted to kill me, and I for sure was not going to climb down there to see if he changed his mind. That was close enough for me!

Chapter 11

Himmler's Limousine

Who is rich? He that is content.
Who is that? Nobody.
Benjamin Franklin
1706-1790

Soon the war would be over. The date: April 1944. My outfit moved from location to location in Germany, stopping in Kassel for a couple of weeks. Now, Kassel was a Nazi town where the people had a real hatred for Americans. I guess they had a reason; our bombers had leveled their fine city.

I confiscated a very large German BMW 4-cylinder motorbike. While riding my big bike up the Autobahn, I decided to venture off into a small city, known as a dorf in Germany.

As I neared the city, I could see people scurrying about and by the time I reached the top, there stood a group of very scared residents out of breath, lined up behind the burgermeister, who was dressed in formal garb, complete with top hat in hand. It was formal, I tell you! He said through an interpreter that the city was mine.

What was I to do? I didn't have my protocol instructions with me, and even if I had them, I had no idea how to complete the transaction. So I smiled and shook hands with many of the group. I'm sure they all thought, 'What a dumb cluck this American is.'

Shortly after that, the Russians were given the town, due to treaties with the Allies. I'm sure all the girls were raped on the night the Russians moved in. These Red Russians were just a grade above savages. They had no education, plus it was payback time for what the Germans had done to Russia.

One day, while riding my bike, a German walked over as I was stopped at a crossroad and spoke in very good English.

"Do you want to buy a car?"

Well, the bike was nice but I had been rained on enough during the war. I parked the bike and dismounted. I then did a whole body search of the German. He was clean. "Lead the way," I said.

He pointed to a garage in an alley. I thought, now is when I meet some armed Nazi sympathizers, so I drew my .45, as he opened the garage door. I couldn't believe my eyes! Parked inside was a jet-black Mercedes Benz limousine with the top down. It was a Phaethon classic!

Then he gave me the history of this magnificent machine. It had belonged to Himmler, who, as most folks know, was the second man in charge of the Nazi government. Himmler ordered the German to park it in the garage for safekeeping. I was still in shock! To my surprise, the gas tank was full, and when I turned it over, it started right up.

You cannot imagine how I felt. Here I was a farm boy from Indiana standing in the passenger seat where Himmler himself stood while viewing the many Nazi military parades that I had seen as a teenager. I was overwhelmed, yet I managed to keep my composure, because the matter of selling price had not been settled. I could have more or less told him to take a hike, but I owed him for choosing me.

I asked him what he wanted for the limousine. "Cigarettes," he replied.

I offered him two cartons of cigarettes, and he simply gave me the keys. We were both very, very happy. I paid two cartons of Camels for the limousine formerly owned by Himmler. Now you might think I came out on top. At the time, cigarettes were selling for around $1000 a carton and before the war, you could buy a new car for that amount but not a limousine, of course.

The sight of me in that limousine caused many hateful eyes from the Nazi sympathizers in town. I was wheeling around in style. Of course, it was full of GIs on every trip I made. Talk about looking like the Beverly Hillbillies; we certainly did!

About the third week in April, we left Kassel and traveled some 60 miles to Worbis, Germany. I was on roadblock duty on the Autobahn. I had a two-man crew. One day a German truck pulled up while I was busy with another truck, so the second truck pulled out and headed down the road. I let him go briefly, then pulled down on him.

The truck was carrying 17 SS troopers. Let me tell you, they wheeled around on a dime and returned. One of them was a civilian, a high Nazi. Out of the truck they came. The civilian came up to me and said if I let him through, he would give me his ring. He showed it to me. Lord, that was one huge diamond!

I was so pissed off seeing evidence of what they had done to the poor people in the concentration camps that I hit him in the mouth with my rifle butt and sent him off to a detention camp. Years later, I saw him on television. He had been captured in South America, so some GI got himself a ring.

A week later, now the end of April, we left Worbis and traveled to Gotha about 40 miles away and set up there. We were in Gotha for about two weeks.

Soon we got our marching orders for Wetzlar, more than 130 miles away. That meant I would have to find someone to ride the bike or leave it, which I wasn't about to do.

Johnny F. Parnel, a kid out of Washington, asked if he could use the bike when he went out on scout duty up the road ahead of the rest of us. We had to travel through the Hartz Mountains, and the road was terrible with sheer cliffs and no guardrails.

Johnny was ordered to report or wait on the convoy every half-hour. I started to worry, when we saw no sign of him or the bike at one point, so I gave the steering wheel to another GI and I stood where Himmler always stood.

As we turned a sharp corner, I caught a glimpse of a reflection down the cliff. I stopped the convoy and the three of us climbed down the cliff not knowing what we would find. Sure enough, there he was 200 feet down, pinned under the 1200-pound bike. It appeared that his hip and leg were crushed. Blood soaked his pant leg from his hip to his shoe. He was screaming in pain. It took all three of us to lift that bike off of Johnny.

[I later learned that a sniper probably shot him in the leg, causing him to lose control of the bike and career down the sheer cliff. That also might explain the excessive bleeding.]

Now, to get him up the cliff! I told him if he didn't wrap his arms around my neck and hold on, he would die, and if he let go, he would surely die, for the drop was another 500 feet. I told him to keep the screams down and bite on my jacket instead.

Somehow he held on and somehow I managed to get enough room to breathe, as he was gripping my neck very tightly almost shutting of my wind. I solved the problem by turning my head to the side.

There was no way the other two GIs with me could have given any additional assistance due to his condition. As we neared the top of the cliff, the other two were there to take him from me.

We always had a medic and an ambulance following our convoy, so it was ordered up front. Once Johnny was in the ambulance, he went to an aid station for treatment. We never knew if he lived or died; he was in such bad shape. As far as I know, the bike is still on the side of that mountain.

I think Himmler would not have been happy to know that his limousine played a part in saving a GI's life, for that is what we did. The convoy made it out of the mountains, and we moved to our new position.

To this day, I have no idea how I mustered the nerve to climb down that sheer cliff, let alone carry a man back up. I will never know how we made it to the top.

One day, I felt a tap on my shoulder. Two MPs were standing behind me. "Where are the keys to the limo?" one of them asked. Rather than get hit upside the head, I handed over the keys. They were acting under orders, so it did no good to give them any lip.

"Who's ordering this?" I asked. They mumbled something about a Major, but I didn't get his name.

Now my bike is on the side of a cliff in the Hartz Mountains, and my limousine is gone, so I went out and stole a Jeep. You could do that back then if the driver left it unguarded. It wasn't the same, though.

[I learned later on that the owner of the Imperial Palace in Las Vegas had the limousine but he died and the car was sold. I think Wayne Newton or Jay Leno has it, but most likely it has been returned to Germany. If I ever meet up with either of them, I'm going to demand that they return it to its rightful owner, as they are in possession of a stolen car. After all, I paid $2000 for it. I wonder what they paid for it!]

Later on, we were in Kassel where I bought Himmler's limousine. Well, George Wargo met up with seven Russian displaced persons and they wanted a drink. By chance, they spotted a doctor's office and broke into it, went to the basement where the doctor stored his wood alcohol, and the party started.

I was in a poker game when the door opened and there stood George with a flashlight in his hand. I don't know if you have ever seen just how big eyeballs can get, but it is huge. As soon as I saw him, I knew they had run into some bad booze. I sort of looked after George. I called a medic, but George died. I went outside and there they lay, the seven Russians – dead!

Our job from then on was to search for weapons. During one such search, I noticed a well in the middle of a field. I walked out to it and pulled off the top of the cistern. I noticed a string tied to a stone. I pulled it up and on the other end was a huge beer stein full of largest diamond rings set in platinum that I had ever seen!

Suddenly a man came running across the field waving his arms and yelling in very good English, "I am the mayor here. All the women in the town gave me their rings for safekeeping."

97

Being from Indiana and dumb as hell, I believed his story and gave him the rings, only to learn that evening that the Mulhausen concentration camp was just a few miles away. The son-of-a-bitch was a surly camp employee, and he had sufficient authority to strip those rings off the poor, helpless women there and not be held accountable.

I grabbed my rifle and was on my way back to kill the bastard, but before I could get away, I heard march orders. We were moving out, so I couldn't complete my plan. I never got the chance to kill him, but oh, how I wanted to!

I know I have a tender heart, because every time I saw those poor women degraded and their poor little girls showing their concentration tattoos, it made my blood boil. If it caught me at the right moment, I would cry. I'm not ashamed to say it. A person had to have been there just to understand how bad it was for the poor people.

Chapter 12

Post-War Service/Regensburg

Every gun that is made, every warship launched,
every rocket fired signifies, in the final sense,
a theft from those who hunger and are not fed,
those who are cold and not clothed.
Dwight D. Eisenhower
1890 - 1969

Wetzlar, Germany

The war was over and it's May 1945. We're in Wetzlar, a city of about 52,000 in west central Germany. I was assigned to search door-to-door for weapons and ammunition. About noon one day, I came across a bombed-out house with only one room left on its second story. A handmade wooden ladder led to that room.

I climbed the ladder, knocked on the door and inside found a terrified woman, alone. I could tell she had class. She was probably about 40 years old, but to a 21-year-old like me, she looked like a grandma.

In broken German, I assured her that I was not there to harm her. Noticing a wall safe, I ordered her to open it, although she begged me not to make her do so.

Inside the safe was a solid gold Leica camera, a gift that her deceased husband had received upon retiring from the company. It was a masterpiece, so heavy that I needed both hands to lift it.

I was concerned about what might happen to the camera, so I insisted that the woman bury it once night fell. Then I moved on to the next house.

[Forty years later, I started to search for the woman and her camera through the Leica Company in Solms, Germany. I explained what happened. "Surely there is a history to this camera that is recorded somewhere," I wrote. "What I'm begging is to know she did not lose it and it's still in her family."

Unfortunately the company professed not to know anything about the story I related or the camera itself. I persisted by writing to the daily newspaper in Wetzlar. A reporter picked up my story and published it.

Finally, in July 1995, the reporter contacted me. He had succeeded in uncovering the rest of the story of the solid gold Leica camera! The camera had survived the looting at the end of the war and the proceeds from its sale went to charity.

"Seen in this light, C. B. Wolfe did a good deed," the reporter wrote, "when he abstained from confiscating the valuable Leica and allowed the woman from Wetzlar to hide the heirloom. That is what you call courage to stand up for your beliefs."

As it turned out, the charity was personal. The woman had a very sick daughter that was hospitalized for many years. From the sale of the camera, she was able to pay for her extensive medical bills.]

Dulag-Luft POW Camp

Next we were assigned to guard the displaced persons camp that the United Nations set up. Considering most of the people in this camp had worked for the Nazis, they knew they could not go back to their homelands or face certain death. This camp, therefore, was a godsend for these poor, homeless men and their families.

Let's assume you have a couple of kids and you're absolutely homeless. This is the first thing that some people could never understand. Surely there would be some organization to give you a hand. Now, you have two scared hungry kids with tears cascading down their cheeks without a whimper. Again, no Red Cross dishing out food. As you walk down the roads, you gathered grass and if you were lucky enough to own a pot, you boiled that grass and that was your food for the day.

God, I'll never forget the look in their eyes that pleaded for anything you could spare. You have absolutely no idea how this affected me.

I was assigned a post, and it was still chilly so I gathered up firewood and built a fire. One evening as I was gathering more wood, a young girl came up with an armload of wood. Now I thought, isn't that sweet? When the fire was throwing out some good heat, we sat down on a makeshift bench I put together. I was amazed that she spoke some English, because up to that time we just sat and watched the flames lick the night air. She told me her family was from Lithuania.

She pointed out where she lived, and I walked her to her place. Before I said good night, I brought out some candy I had for a late night snack and gave it to her. Lord, she was so grateful!

I hoped she would show up the next night. Sure enough, she came with her two younger sisters trailing behind her. We all sat around the fire and tried to understand each other. When I brought out the candy, I noticed they were dividing it and putting some away when they noticed that I was watching. The oldest girl said, "Mommy and Poppy." That meant they were saving a certain portion to give to their parents.

Mind you, not one of the girls ever asked or begged for anything. They had upbringing and class, and even at their young ages it showed.

I knew they were hungry, so I started bringing hot dogs and other food items. Again they always saved a share for Mommy and Poppy. As we got better acquainted, the babies started to get as close to me as they could, and the oldest one would sit on the ground in front of me as close as possible. I had me a family that loved me for me. Lord, did I ever love them back!

I noticed they started showing signs of sadness. This hurt the hell out of me, thinking someone was causing them to feel this way. The oldest daughter told me that her father had a hand grenade, and he was going to kill all of them as soon as they were ordered back to Lithuania. I thought surely he wouldn't kill those sweet loving girls, but I reported it and hoped someone would inspect their room.

The girls were so sad. The next night, they didn't come to see me. Then I heard it. BOOM! The grenade exploded. I ran to the room where they lived and without knocking, I swung open the door and there on the floor lay the five of them, dead.

The father had gathered them all in a circle on the floor, with the grenade in the center so that they all received the same force of the explosion. He wanted to make sure of that, so there were no survivors.

I can't describe the sight or my feelings. To this day, I'm still not over it, and tears well in my eyes as I think about those precious girls dead at such innocent ages.

Rosie

We moved to a mountain village that had very few people but a lot of geese and pigs. Oh, yes, there was a bar with plenty of fights, many of which involved me. I believe there were no more than three girls in the whole town.

One day I noticed a girl that didn't seem to belong there. She was dressed very nice and was very pretty. Her name was Rosie. We hit it right off.

Rosie was the reason for so many fights, simply because she was so beautiful. One woman and 145 woman-starved men who had their sights set on her. She followed me wherever I went.

I learned that she was Swiss and had worked as an entertainer for the German troops and married an SS officer, who was killed. The Swiss wouldn't allow her to return home, so she was looking for a place to settle down.

A few days later, I spotted a huge house all fenced in, which is normal for German farmhouses. I knocked until my knuckles were raw. Suddenly, a very scared lady opened the door, so I told Rosie what to say.

"This young lady needs a place to live and I won't take no for an answer."

The woman was shaking from fear but finally invited us in. It was her first encounter with an American.

We walked up the stairs, and she pointed out the room where Rosie could stay. Rosie was overjoyed, because she had been prepared to sleep in the bushes along the road.

Again, using her as an interpreter, I laid down the law. The lady even offered me lunch, but I refused because food back then was nearly impossible to get, but Rosie ate. She was so starved that she gulped the food down fast, nearly choking in the process.

You cannot fathom what it was like being without food. I found it strange that I never saw dogs or cats. Hell, they probably ate them!

At the time, my job was distributing food to the other batteries, so they ate well. I did not know it but all this time the owner's son was hiding out in the farmhouse, as he had deserted his army. It didn't make much difference, as the German army was done anyway.

Regensburg

The 134th Battalion was approaching its 2nd anniversary. Our next move was to Regensburg, Germany, where we would stay briefly. Before leaving, I made sure Rosie had money, food and a train ticket so we could meet up again. We actually rode the German train part way to Regensburg, then I transferred to another mode of transportation, and Rosie continued on the train.

The main reason for going to Regensburg was to celebrate the 2nd anniversary of the 134th and the end of the war. By some unexplained set of circumstances, it would once again put me face to face with Colonel Israel, the man who rescued me from behind enemy lines just a few months earlier.

The event was held June 11, because the actual anniversary fell on a Sunday. We called it a celebration of our organization as an outfit.

The day began with a rousing parade to the marches of the 70th Infantry Division band brought to Regensburg for this occasion. Brigadier General Timberlake and his staff were on hand and made speeches after the parade. As Richard Flora so aptly wrote in the 134th Madcap Memories journal, "General Timberlake will long be remembered for his rugged humor and witty personality."

The afternoon was spent playing softball games. In the evening, a raffle was held. I won first prize – a Speed Graphic camera, and Colonel Israel won a solid gold Rolex Oyster Perpetual watch.

The Colonel approached me immediately after the prizes were awarded and asked if I would be willing to trade with him, as he really wanted the camera. I told him that after what he did saving our lives, he could keep both, but being the great man that he was, he merely chuckled and handed me the watch.

That was the last time I saw him. I don't know if he received a medal for his bravery on that mission, but I rather doubt it. At least, I was able to shake his hand, look him in the eye and say, "Thank you, Colonel."

I kept the watch for a long time and eventually sold it to a collector in Indianapolis.

Deactivation

It is now the summer of 1945. The 134th AAA Battalion was ordered to move again, but this time back to the United States. Almost all of the troops that had earned their points returned home. Hell, I didn't want to go home, so I agreed to stay. I really didn't have a home to return to, anyway, as my mother and father were nearly 80.

Three GIs, an officer and I stayed behind to dispose of all the material. Considering I was Chief of Quartermaster, I had to find a safe area to hide 15 2½-ton Army trucks fully loaded with 90mm shells. In addition, I had to dispose of small arms ammo, hand grenades and bazooka projectiles.

V Corps had been shipping 90mm shells to me because I had storage space. My inventory had grown to over 12,000 rounds of these shells. To those who don't know, the copper alone in each of these shells weighs 37 pounds, not including the projectile and powder.

We're talking millions of dollars in scrap buried in Germany. The 444,000 pounds of copper at $2/pound alone means almost a million dollars, plus the powder used to put the fizz in soft drinks. Then there is the projectile. The German government could salvage this and still come out ahead.

The stash would make at least 3000 bombs, as they strap four together. This makes on hell of an explosion, with the potential of killing thousands. To the best of my knowledge, despite my attempts to notify the German government of this stash, it is still in place.

Anyway, I called the Quartermaster at V Corps and informed him we were deactivating and asked when I should send the shells back.

"Do not send them back and that's an order!" he barked in no uncertain terms.

"What should I do with them and the other ammo in the inventory?"

"I don't give a goddamn!" he fumed. "Just do not send them back."

I could not abandon the inventory, so alone I started to search for a safe location to hide all of the equipment and weapons. It took me two weeks to find the right spot.

I called the United Nations and asked them to send me some displaced persons. They sent out 28 Polish men. Without a doubt these were the most intelligent men I had ever met.

I had my cooks prepare anything these men wanted to eat for their breakfast. There was steak, eggs and pork chops – the works, including fresh coffee.

I noticed, however, that the men were just nibbling at this incredible feast, and when I asked why, they said the food was fine, but their stomachs had shrunk due to the starvation diet in the concentration camps. Hearing this I felt terrible for them and for all the suffering they had endured.

Now I feared they wouldn't have the energy to do the loading and unloading, so I told them if they felt weak and couldn't go on, to let me know and we would continue the next day. It was damp and chilly, and they were dressed poorly. I had to do something, so I broke out heavy duty boots, socks, underwear, pants, shirts and parkas. I had me 28 men that looked like GIs. You wouldn't believe how happy they were to be treated like human beings again.

The loading completed, we fired up the engines and were off into the darkness of early morning. We had no problem reaching the location I selected for dumping. I wasn't at all surprised that we saw no Germans on the go during the unloading or in the darkness returning to the compound, because the Germans had no gas or cars, and we were the only Americans within 25 miles.

When we returned to the compound, I noticed that the United Nations trucks were waiting, and the convoy commander was wringing his hands.

"What the hell is going on here?" I demanded. "These men are hungry and my cooks have food waiting."

He very excitedly said that his orders were to pick up the men and deliver them to Helmstedt where a train would be would be waiting to take them to Poland. He said they were Stalin's orders and if he didn't get them there on time, he would lose his job, and these men would not be returned home until a much later date.

Dumb ass me, I bought the lie. "All right, just as soon as I feed them."

The commander again became frantic, and the men said it was all right, as they wanted to go home. The commander directed them to the waiting trucks.

I turned to the men to say goodbye and thank you, but I noticed they weren't happy. I'm sure now that they knew it was a lie, too.

The next day the convoy commander came back to our compound and told me what happened. When they reached Helmstedt, a company of Russian troops was lined up like they were on parade, only it was no parade.

As the men left the train, the Russians ripped off all their clothes. Stealing clothes was an old Russian trick. They then marched the men, now crying, to a prepared grave and shot them all.

You have no idea how I felt. I even wanted to kill the UN convoy commander, because he knew how the Reds operated. I managed to restrain myself.

[I later wrote to the Polish Ambassador, explaining what took place. I tried to pinpoint the location of the pit, and he was most grateful for my feelings. He sent a gift to me out of gratitude, which I thought was very nice. I wanted those men to be returned home for proper burial. I told him that it was early summer and that sadly the new grass had covered any evidence of a gravesite.]

One day I was called into the battalion office and questioned about my combat experience. It seems they were looking for a man, who had been in combat, to lead a platoon of men and one Captain to guard a trainload of material containing the records and leaders of the German government. That meant, if there was to be any firing, I was the one to do it if the Russians stopped the train as we were transferring the records to Berlin.

We received orders to guard the movement of the German government documents and high-ranking personnel from Hessisch Lictenau to Berlin. I never ever thought I would meet up with the firing squad that killed these great men and good friends.

At the Helmstedt roadblock, we all looked out the train windows to see why we stopped where the Polish men had been murdered a short time earlier. The Russians had stopped the train and insisted on breaking the padlocked boxcars.

As soon as I saw them, I knew it was the same firing squad. I reported to the Captain in charge and said if they gave us any trouble, I would shoot to kill. I was the only one with combat experience, and the other five men, including the Captain, were scared to death.

Many of the German government leaders had crawled under their seats and were crying out, "They will kill me! Don't let them board the train!"

I wasn't afraid. I just wanted to even the score for what they had done earlier. It hadn't been long since I was in combat, so I still had that kill mentality. My weapon was a Thompson machine gun. They had machine guns, too, but I knew I could take a few of them out.

As I walked out onto the platform, a Russian soldier walked up with a bolt cutter to cut the lock. I flipped the safety off and pointed the gun at his head. Then I noticed a man who must have been their officer in charge yell out an order, so I just turned and trained the muzzle of my gun on his forehead.

I saw his jaw muscle quiver, and it seemed like we stood there for 15 minutes before he gave the order to back off. Nothing more was said, and the guard stood at attention.

This had an immediate effect, because the commander gave another order and the soldier fell back into the ranks. I had my chance, and oh, how I wanted to pull that trigger. I realized if I opened fire we all would have died, and it could have caused the outbreak of World War III right then and there, as we had many Germans on the train.

When I was finally relieved, I instructed my relief to pull down on the leader; he would know him because he was the one with the big mouth. After 48 hours, the Russians pulled back.

As I returned to the train, many of the German leaders were crying and hugging me – even kissing me – which had never happened to me before. They had been terrified that this Russian firing squad would find them and kill them.

Jail break

We were stationed on the side of a mountain used by the Germans to shoot off gliders into the valley below. Five of us were involved in this story – Donald "Smitty" Smith, William Miller, Melvin Delvige (a big Texas), John Finegan and me.

The villagers locked all their girls at home, which was apparent, because there were no girls running around. These guys hit on Rosie whenever I wasn't around. The little devil didn't help matters, because she was a showgirl and before closing the only bar in this woman-less dorf, she would climb up on the bar and do a striptease. Of course, this only added to the misery these guys felt.

We all had Jeeps. Smitty had to go over the mountain to get a girl, and while he was making out with her, the girl's brother took Smitty's Jeep out for a spin. Well, this kid couldn't drive a duck to water, and he ended up hitting a kid on a bicycle, killing him.

The German night watchman arrested Smitty, and some son-of-a-bitch sent him to the stockade in Heidelburg. Well, we surely had ourselves a problem. How do we spring Smitty?

There was a lieutenant over us, but as far as he was concerned, the war was over and it was time to party. We seldom saw him and when we did, it was just "How are you boys doing?"

We would say, "Great", and he, in turn, would salute and say, "Carry on." Boy, did we ever!

We came up with a plan to spring Smitty. We would engage a German woman to sew sergeant's stripes on Delvige's jacket. He already had the appearance of getting the hell kicked out of him in every fight he was ever in. We chose him to be the leader of the pack on this rescue mission.

In the stockroom, we found helmets with MP painted on them, plus other documents that we could use to prove we were MPs. With all the papers in order, we took off for Heidelburg.

After a long drive, we arrived at the prison. With all of the authority we could muster, we banged on the door of the Provost Marshal's office. We introduced ourselves and informed him that we had orders to pick up a prisoner.

With bloodshot eyes, the officer looked up at us. I'm sure we were all thinking the same thing, 'How can we all fit through this door if he sees through our scheme?' Thank God, we all stood our ground. This man had one hell of a hangover and wanted us out of there just as badly as we wanted out.

Shortly afterward, here came a guard with a worried looking Smitty in tow. He played the part like a movie star. I slapped the cuffs on him and someone shoved him through the door.

We made no careless moves until we were a mile away, then all hell broke loose, yelling and laughing. Suddenly Smitty said, "Take these f--king cuffs off!" We had forgotten to remove the handcuffs. Now Smitty was free.

He made up some kind of excuse to the local police and there was no further investigation. I laugh every time I think of how comical we all were in this situation.

1st Infantry

Next, I served with the 1st Infantry. I was assigned as a chaperone for Sgt. Wood. He had just come off duty as the chief hangman of the Nazis. Hanging was too good for those sons-of-bitches. I'm sure Sgt. Wood had no knowledge of the terrible treatment and killings these bastards had committed. I believe I was placed with him as a guard because command thought he was a marked man.

He was truly a mess, dirty and unshaven for over a week. He was drunk all the time, and the Army brought him cases of whiskey on a regular basis. I guess Wood felt obligated to consume it all.

He had fallen out of the bed so often, they put his sleeping bag on the floor, and that's where he slept. He soiled himself all the time, and other personnel would come in and clean him up. He smelled terrible.

Sgt. Wood slept with two .45 pistols cocked at all times in their holsters. This I didn't like and I made it known to the CO, but he would not do anything to upset Wood.

After a few days, he sobered up enough to talk. I asked him about the hangings and he didn't want to talk about them, but he did tell me he hated Striker, and when he placed him on the platform to drop him through, he placed him so the drop would take his nose off.

Now, either Wood missed the mark or Striker's nose was sewn back on because years later, on the History Channel, I saw a picture of dead Nazis on the floor, and Striker's nose was still intact.

I knew sooner or later Sgt. Wood would draw down on me in one of his drunken fits and one of us would be dead, because I was also packing cocked .45s. I had my fill of it and requested a transfer.

The placement officer told me to pack up and off I went in a Jeep to my new assignment. If I'm not mistaken, Sgt. Wood was dead shortly after I was assigned to manage the brewery in Regensburg.

The local bishop owned the brewery. We did one hell of a business, selling $30,000 to $40,000 worth of the suds each day. It seems the GIs had a taste for that beer. That became a bore, however, as I did very little drinking.

Going home

My time in the service was about to end. The Army contacted me that my father was gravely ill. I signed a contract with the Army Exchange that I would return as a civilian manager of service clubs in Germany.

It was time to say goodbye to Rosie. I was so young with nothing to offer, and I wasn't ready to get married. So with tears in my eyes and holding her tightly, I told her the story and kissed her goodbye. Her face was as covered with tears as mine was. What a sad parting! I wouldn't wish it on anyone.

I returned to the States, where I was honorably discharged and returned to civilian life for eight months. During that time, my father died and I moved to Michigan.

Chapter 13

Back to Regensburg

When the candles are out,
all women are fair.
Plutarch
46 AD - 120 AD

When I returned to Regensburg, I attended school to brush up on club management. In my free time, I went up and down the streets looking for Rosie, but I never found her.

I managed Army Exchange services, posts with restaurants, movie theaters and social clubs. My first club assignment was the Red Cross Service Club working with the Red Cross girls. Well, at last I was in heaven!

There were 64 girls, all in their 20s, and six very eager Red Cross girls. These girls were forbidden to leave the building, as we furnished living quarters. If they were caught outside they were fired on the spot, because there was so much VD, we couldn't chance spreading it around.

The girls, the commanding officer (CO) of the troops stationed in Regensburg and I all lived on the third floor of the club. The CO was dating one of the Red Cross girls. Even the Red Cross girls could not have their boyfriends on the third floor. Of course, I was hit on 24/7.

Pure heaven: No men, only young girls free of VD. They were given a weekly check up. There was no problem if one of them got pregnant, because the girls all wanted a baby and made every effort to become pregnant. I also made every effort. I learned a man can overdo such daily and nightly action because it soon became extremely difficult to urinate.

I rushed to the doctor and told him he surely missed one of the girls because I thought I had a double dose of the clap! He laid his head on his desk and his shoulders shook as he laughed.

In between gasps for air, he begged me, "Throw a rope out the window so I can climb up and spend a night in your heaven." When his laughing convulsions stopped, he offered me $500 and said he would furnish the rope.

This experience taught me about overdoing a good thing. I lost 20 pounds, and I could not afford to lose that much at 6'2" and 160 pounds. I looked like one of the concentration camp victims at 140 pounds!

I had a big problem. The Colonel came every night to be with a Red Cross girl, and I mean he was a drunk. Seems that's all he lived for – drinking. I really doubt if he and the girl ever had sex.

Well, every night it was my duty to carry him down three flights of stairs, dump him in his command car, bumping the back of his head with a loud thud, closing the door, and away he and his driver went. This was an every night occurrence.

Every night, there standing naked was his girlfriend waiting on me. By that time I was simply scored out because I had assigned the girls when it was time to come to my room. I started wondering if the undertaker could wipe the smile off my face from screwing myself to death.

This experience may be hard to believe but one must remember these girls had never been with a man in their lives, and a good portion had never been screwed, and they all wanted to have babies. I must admit after a while, it was no longer fun! It turned out to be a daily job.

I had one girl, whom they all claimed was a Russian countess, and she had class. I was amazed that she somehow escaped with all her diamonds, and they were huge. She was my favorite. The problem was, she also had a girl with her that took care of her sexual needs when I was busy.

She was well trained to satisfy a man, though. I remember her skin; it was so white and soft. I was in heaven, and the great part was I knew it! You know, as I look back on my life I have had experiences that only rulers of a large nation enjoy!

Landshut, Germany

Next stop: Landshut, 60 miles away. Romance blossomed for me once again, this time with a German girl, a native of Landshut by the name of Charlotte.

We met on a blind date. It was a double date with a Major. He and Charlotte, his date, were in the front seat, and my date and I were in the back seat. While we were going wherever we were going, Charlotte reached back and held my hand the whole time. Our romance started budding that day.

We were married right there in Landshut, but we didn't have any choice about staying there or leaving. Back then, according to American law if you married a German national, you could not stay in Germany, so Charlotte and I came to the United States in 1951. We settled down and were blessed with two wonderful daughters, Donna and Darlene.

Chapter 14

Afterthoughts

Captain Foley

From the time I promised Captain Foley that I would keep the Glenn Miller tragedy a secret between the two of us, I harbored feelings that he wanted me dead, perhaps to eliminate any possibility that I would eventually snitch or, worse, blackmail him.

If I had spilled the beans, he most likely would have lost his commission. Going from Captain to buck private was the worst thing that could happen to an officer. I think that fear led him to tell me, "Shut your goddamned mouth."

There were a few incidents that had me convinced until recently that Captain Foley wanted me dead. First, when we landed on the beach in Normandy, where there were thousands of unexploded shells that should have been neutralized by Army experts. Who did the Captain give the job to? Yours truly. I was lucky to live through that experience.

Second, before the Battle of the Bulge started, Captain Foley ordered me to go with another GI on a scouting mission three miles behind enemy lines. Everyone – including the Captain – knew this was Wafen SS territory. If the SS had not been ordered to keep hidden and silent, the two of us would have been killed, no questions asked.

Third, Battery D pulled out without telling three other men and me that they were leaving. As the SS advanced, we were trapped far behind in enemy territory with little hope of being rescued, and when we were finally brought back to our outfit, the Captain didn't even say howdy.

I do not recall ever seeing Captain Foley sober during the war. He certainly lived up to a good Irish drinking reputation, and he had plenty of assistance with whiskey rations on a monthly basis.

Now, in no way do I state this observation to malign his character or to hurt his surviving family members. However, his drinking most likely impaired his decision making, from the shooting down of Glenn Miller's plane (and claiming he was calibrating the guns instead) to putting me in high-risk jobs that could have gotten me killed.

The problem I faced in mentioning his drinking habit was that I had no corroboration. Not until, thanks to my editor's perseverance, we contacted Captain Foley's former driver, Gilbert "Gibby" Davis.

Gibby clearly recalls that Captain Foley had a drinking problem. In recollecting that fact, he related, first to me and then to my editor, an experience that he and the Captain had when they were out driving around one day. That particular day Captain Foley was more than a little tipsy. He ordered Gibby to make a turn up ahead. Gibby told him that he could not make that turn, as it would put them on railroad tracks.

"Shut your damn mouth!" he ordered Gibby. [Déjà vu all over again, as Yogi Berra would say!]

So, being a dutiful soldier, Gibby made the turn, only to have the Jeep get stuck on the tracks. Before he left to get help quite some distance away, Captain Foley gave him another order, not to tell anyone that he had given that order. That's exactly how he handled me in the Miller incident.

Now, as I look back and re-evaluate the Captain in a new light, I have changed my thoughts about his intentions. Drunk or sober, Captain Foley was correct to order the guns to fire on a lone plane with no IFF.

When the Captain ordered the secret between us about that shooting, I would like to believe maybe it was not just because he had had too much to drink but because, like me, he loved Glenn Miller's music and hated the thought that he had participated in Miller's demise. Perhaps keeping me out of sight, like on those remote dangerous missions, gave him some rest from that horrible memory.

I still regret that I reported the "No IFF" data to him. I'm sure if I had held this information back; the Captain might never have given the order to shoot. We both did the jobs that were expected of us.

Another thought comes to mind. Commanding officers would always call out the man they trusted to do a job properly. Could it be that was the case when Captain Foley sent me on those high-risk assignments? I'm beginning to think that could very well be the case. I was fearless and conscientious about doing my job.

Example: Going behind enemy lines to snoop around and bringing back the information about the hob-nail boot tracks and tank tracks, giving Battery D time to move out or the whole outfit would have been added to the massacre that the 106th suffered.

Another example: Sending my M-51 Quad up to the Ludendorff bridgehead to be the only gun there right after the bridge was taken. He knew I would do my best, and it worked out well, didn't it?

I now wish I had been able to see Captain Foley in peaceful times. I understand he had a wonderful sense of humor and was quite the storyteller. I would like to have told him to his face that there was never any chance I would have revealed our secret or blackmailed him. It's just not in my character to do something like that.

I would also like to believe that Captain Foley would understand why I am breaking my promise to him now. He would respect the responsibility to history that he and I shared and that now I am in a position to deliver.

Colonel Israel

For years, I have tried to locate Colonel Israel. I wanted to thank him again for saving my life. I also wanted to make sure that he received a medal for the bravery he demonstrated rescuing the three of us from behind enemy lines in December 1944. Unfortunately, I have never found him. No one in our battery has ever heard of him. That still plagues me.

While putting together materials for this book, however, and talking to some of the survivors of the 134th, such as Pete Hall and Ed Shanahan, who were assigned to headquarters, I learned something that made me give up my search for Colonel Israel. Hall and Shanahan convinced me that the Colonel must have belonged to G2 (Intelligence).

In fact, Hall said that a colonel happened to be at battery headquarters at the beginning of the Bulge. "Get your unit out of here!" the colonel ordered in an urgent tone.

"I do not know who that colonel was. All I know is that we were ahead of the 106th Infantry and the tanks were going to overrun us," said Hall. Could that colonel have been Colonel Israel? It sounds like it. Colonel Israel cared about saving the lives of the men in our unit, and he was willing to risk his life doing so.

The G2 angle fits for several reasons. First, there is just no way a normal battalion commander would have the training or nerve to undertake such a rescue mission. It would have been pure suicide for an untrained person to drive behind enemy lines through all those SS roadblocks. One slip and we would have all been dead – or worse yet, he would have been killed en route to our dugout.

The Germans all carried "papers" and when stopped they reached for these papers. Now where would a battalion commander come up with "papers" like that on short notice? Of course, G2 had them all made up for their spies in the field. These surely were done properly because no one would want to risk raising any suspicion in the SS troopers at the checkpoints.

Of course, the three of us were under those frozen bodies. Every stop we feared was our last, but the Colonel really ripped into these SS guards. The other clue that he was G2 was his ability to speak perfect German, which would have been unlikely of regular commanders.

It all makes sense now. I still wish I could find out if he received a medal for heroism. He was an incredibly brave and fearless man, bound by duty to his GIs.

Mysterious morning reports

After the manuscript for this book was finished, the long awaited morning reports, filed by Captain Foley each day for the previous day's activities, came through. I was particularly interested in seeing if those reports noted that three of us were missing (from the night of December 16th to perhaps the 21st) or that we were rescued.

In a way, it came as no surprise that no mention of either appears in the morning reports. The captain wrote that Delaney was missing, but then scratched out that remark on the report of December 19th. I suspect that, as the captain was filling out his morning report that day, Delaney returned to the unit.

Why did the captain not mention that three other men were missing? Why did he – on a subsequent report – not mention the colonel's rescue and our return to the unit? Perhaps he didn't for the same reason he didn't come out to greet us upon our return.

One thing I did learn from these hard-to-obtain morning reports was where Battery D was located when Colonel Israel returned us. It was Sourbrodt, Belgium, just 13.9 miles from Losheim, where he rescued us.

Those 13.9 miles seemed like the 50 miles that someone told us we had traveled, but perhaps the distance really was longer because Colonel Israel might have taken a circuitous route to Sourbrodt to avoid certain SS checkpoints. Anyway, I guess being buried under frozen dead bodies would make any trip seem longer than it is.

Weapons stash

I returned to Germany twice since the end of the war and on the first trip, I drove to the dumpsite where I buried the live ammunition, only to find the area completely undisturbed.

On my second trip to Germany, I again returned to the site and was not surprised to see it still undisturbed. By then, though, many trees had grown, which meant the site was still intact.

Before I die, I am determined to show this site to someone and make sure it is dismantled, because even after all these years the nitro in the gunpowder is highly volatile and would blow at a mere touch. I have contacted the German government five times about this buried ammunition. Apparently they are not interested in having me show them the dumpsite.

At one point, I met with the former superintendent of the Bridgeport Bass, the factory that manufactured the 90mm shell casings that we used in the war. According to him, the United States government ordered these casings made of pure copper. Each casing contained 37 pounds of copper! That's a lot of money!

Glenn Miller

To the Glenn Miller fans across the globe, I sincerely hope that my forthrightness will finally put to rest the mystery of what really happened to the man that captured the hearts of lonely young men fighting a terrible war far from home. As I often said to my editor while putting my memories on paper, I believe Glenn Miller was helping us, as we found just what we needed to validate my memories, even after 62 years.

Regardless the circumstances of his death, we must remember his life and his great contributions to World War II. As for me, his music has remained a part of my life all these years, as it will always be.

Inquiry

Finally, I hope that a formal inquiry into the death of Glenn Miller would be forthcoming and that the United States Army and Air Force would either prove me wrong or admit that my memories are correct about what happened on that fateful day – September 9, 1944.

Printed in the United States
128702LV00008B/325/A

9 781425 969509